Introduction to

YOUTH JUSTICE

incorporating *An Introduction to the Youth Court*

Winston Gordon
Philip Cuddy
Jonathan Black

Foreword to the First Edition by
Lord Woolf of Barnes, Master of the Rolls

Under the auspices of the
Justices' Clerks Society

Editor Bryan Gibson

SECOND EDITION

WATERSIDE PRESS
WINCHESTER

The authors

Winston Gordon is Justices' Clerk, Justices' Chief Executive and Training Officer for Tameside, Greater Manchester. He is a member of the Executive Committee of the Justices' Clerks' Society Standing Committee of Magistrates' Training Officers and a member of the Duchy of Lancaster Branch Training Committee. He is a solicitor—with experience of prosecuting and defending in the magistrates' court—and a member of the Society's Criminal Law Network.

Philip Cuddy is Justices' Clerk and Justices' Chief Executive for Stockport, Greater Manchester. He is a solicitor and has held four separate appointments as Justices' Clerk. As Training Officer he has contributed to events in many different regions. He is a member of the Standing Committee of Magistrates' Training Officers, and was a founder member of the Youth Justice Steering Group for Greater Manchester.

Jonathan Black is Justices' Clerk and Director of Legal Services for Hampshire. He is a solicitor and has a masters degree in criminal justice. He is the Justices' Training Manager for Hampshire and has been involved in the delivery of training in many areas of the country. He was a member of the Home Secretary's Task Force on Youth Justice and is a member of the Youth Justice Board for England and Wales.

Editor

Bryan Gibson is a barrister-at-law and was for 17 years a Clerk to the Justices in Hampshire—when he also served on the council of the Justices' Clerks' Society and as legal adviser to the Magistrates' Association Sentencing of Offenders Committee. He is a former co-editor of the weekly journal *Justice of the Peace* and is now a full-time author, editor and publisher of such works as *Introduction to the Criminal Justice Process* (1995), *The Sentence of the Court* series (1996 to 1999), *The Magistrates Bench Handbook* (1998) and *The Prisons Handbook* (1998).

Introduction to

YOUTH JUSTICE

incorporating *An Introduction to the Youth Court*

A basic outline of the arrangements for youth justice in England and Wales, including the law, practice and sentencing powers of the youth court, produced under the auspices of the Justices' Clerks' Society for use by youth panel magistrates and other people concerned with the provision of youth justice services.

SECOND EDITION

Introduction to **Youth Justice**
incorporating *An Introduction to the Youth Court*

SECOND EDITION

Published 1999 by
WATERSIDE PRESS
Domum Road
Winchester SO23 9NN
Telephone or Fax 01962 855567
E-mail:watersidepress@compuserve.com

First reprint 2000

ISBN Paperback 1 872 870 75 9

Cataloguing-in-Publication Data A catalogue record for this book can be obtained from the British Library.

Printing and binding Antony Rowe Ltd, Chippenham

Cover design John Good Holbrook Ltd, Coventry. Using repeat images of a painting by Peter Cameron entitled 'Troubled Youth'. The original is reproduced to the right. Peter Cameron started painting whilst serving a ten and a half year prison sentence and came to terms with his imprisonment by making it the subject of his art. He is now a freelance artist and can be contacted at The Hub, 9-13 Berry Street, Liverpool. Telephone 0151 709 0889.

First edition *Introduction to the Youth Court,* incorporating *The Sentence of the Youth Court,* published by Waterside Press, 1996, ISBN 1 872 870 36 8.

Introduction to Youth Justice is one of a series of introductory publications designed for newcomers or people who need a concise overview and ready source of reference. Some further details appear at the end of this work.

Introduction to **Youth Justice**

CONTENTS

PART TWO: See overleaf

PART TWO

CHAPTER

8 Sentences & Orders of the Youth Court 92

PART THREE

CHARTS

Foreword to the First Edition

The Right Honourable Lord Woolf of Barnes
Master of the Rolls

The contribution of Justices and their Clerks to the administration of justice is, of course, immense. The way in which their contribution is most demanding and of the greatest importance is, however, in relation to youngsters including young offenders. When exercising their jurisdiction in the Youth Court the decisions of Magistrates can result in youngsters mending their ways or being confirmed on a course of increasingly serious repetitive offending, at least during their teens and into early adult life. The cost of the latter pattern of behaviour on them and on society is so great that it is difficult to measure. Today, there is rightly a wide range of alternative methods of disposal available within the Youth Court. There are also strict procedural guidelines to be followed. Those Magistrates who have the great responsibility of exercising the jurisdiction of the Youth Court need all the help they can obtain while doing so. They need training and the quality of the training is continuing to improve all the time. They also need a reference book to which they can turn to support and supplement that training and in order to refresh their recollection of what they have already learnt. That reference book has to be clearly expressed and readily understandable. It has also to be reasonably compact but still comprehensive, without being intimidating. It must be accurate. 'Introduction to the Youth Court'* fulfils all these requirements. I congratulate the three experienced Justices' Clerks who are the authors, for writing this book and the Justices' Clerks' Society for promoting its publication. It provides just the support members of the Youth Court panels require.

* The title of the First Edition

Aims, Objectives and Preliminary Notes

This handbook was compiled under the auspices of the Justices' Clerks' Society by three experienced training officers to magistrates. The intentions were:

- to provide a companion for new members of the youth panel as they undertake their training
- to assist trainers by allowing them to concentrate on imparting skills necessary for making informed, balanced and structured decisions — in the knowledge that background material can be found in the handbook
- to provide an accessible reference point for youth panel magistrates
- to inform other court users and students about relevant procedures and evidential provisions, and about how decisions are approached in the youth court
- to produce a lucid account, avoiding jargon and complexity. Statutory and other references — the province of court legal advisers and other lawyers — are not reproduced unless especially significant or where they are in common, everyday use. *The handbook cannot replace legal advice, which should be sought in all but the most straightforward cases.*

Wider purpose

This edition has been extended to provide a brief outline of the responsibilities of other people involved in the youth justice process — a further aim being that they (and the general public) may find the materials useful. *Part I* of *Introduction to Youth Justice* now includes an overview of the general principles which underpin youth justice, including the responsibilites of youth offending teams (YOTs), the police and local authorities — following the Crime and Disorder Act 1998, have fresh statutory responsibilities (and with more likely to follow).

Part II contains a comprehensive outline of the sentences and other orders available to the youth court for offenders below the age of 18, whilst *Part III* consists of a number of explanatory charts.

Preliminary Notes

The handbook deals with the special rules which affect *juveniles*, i.e. people aged ten to 17 years inclusive but not yet 18. Many underlying principles are the same as for adults but, where appropriate, more general rules are summarised. They are set out more fully in *The Sentence of the Court* (Waterside Press, 1998).

We have aimed to describe youth justice as at today's date, taking account of a changing situation, phased implementation of the 1998 Act and the existence of a number of pilot schemes. Throughout the text, a 'helping hand' symbol (📖 ✋) is used to identify areas where further advice or information — beyond what can be included in a basic handbook (and including the future timing of certain changes) — is recommended.

Bryan Gibson, Editor
1 February 1999

CHAPTER 1

Introduction and General Outline

A proper understanding of youth justice requires an awareness which goes well beyond the letter of the law. Much of the subject is grounded in developments which have occurred over a long period of time, during which a special 'ethos' has become attached to work with young people who are in conflict with the law. Historically, this so-called ethos has stemmed from efforts to balance the need for a firm response to offending (some criminal offences can, after all, be very serious) with welfare considerations. This latter aspect means that allowances can be made by people at all stages of the youth justice process to reflect differences, e.g. in levels of maturity and intellect, degrees of parental guidance or control, and other imbalances which may have affected an individual child's development or behaviour.

Legislative measures affecting juveniles extend from the early part of the twentieth century through some highly innovative developments (notably of the 1960s, 1970s and 1980s) to what, as the year 2000 approaches, the present government would describe as methods designed to be 'tough on crime, tough on the causes of crime' (the legal framework for which is contained primarily in the Crime and Disorder Act 1998). Indeed, this edition of *Introduction to Youth Justice* appears at a time of change, involving phased implementation of the 1998 Act and a number of pilot schemes designed to test the new provisions—at a key moment, when youth courts and youth justice practitioners will be directly involved in determining how, exactly, youth justice achieves its new direction.

Certain items from the past are undoubtedly redundant (the former practice of repeatedly giving an offender a police caution is an example: *Chapter 3*), whilst others with a solid pedigree in existing youth justice practice have become central to official policy—such as multi-agency working, 'action plans' for offenders, and greater parental and community involvement. It will also be necessary to consider how the new principal statutory aim of youth justice—preventing offending (p. 13)—is to be reconciled with the kind of welfare considerations mentioned above.

YOUTH JUSTICE: ORIGINS & DEVELOPMENT

It was not until 1908 that Parliament fully recognised the desirability of making special arrangements to cater for criminal cases involving younger offenders—a comparatively late development in terms of the evolution of the courts in England and Wales. The Children Act 1908 established 'juvenile courts' and this proved to be the first of many initiatives through which such offenders were separated from their older counterparts and dealt with in a way more appropriate to their age, needs and understanding.

The juvenile court continued until 1992 when, under the Criminal Justice Act 1991, it was transformed into the modern-day 'youth court'. The 1908 Act marked the start of a series of developments in relation to the sentencing of young people. It abolished imprisonment for offenders under 14 years of age and introduced criteria to restrict imprisonment for those aged 14 to 16 years inclusive—whilst the then newly-formed juvenile court dealt with offenders aged eight to 15 years inclusive. Under the Children and Young Persons Act 1963 (CYPA 1963) the age of criminal responsibility was raised from eight to ten years and the upper age limit for the juvenile court extended by a year so that it then dealt with people aged ten to 16 years, but not yet 17.

Although the 1908 Act created the juvenile court, the CYPA 1933, 1963 and 1969 established the foundations and special ethos (already mentioned) of the jurisdiction—on which the Criminal Justice Act 1991 built when it gave the court its current name and raised the upper age limit to include 17-year-olds.

The welfare principle

Many tenets of the 1933 Act still underpin thinking in the youth court, notably the 'welfare principle' whereby, when sentencing, courts look beyond the offending and also consider the longer term development of the individual:

> Every court in dealing with a child or young person who is brought before it, either as an offender or otherwise, shall have regard to the welfare of the child or young person, and shall in a proper case take steps for removing him from undesirable surroundings, and for securing that proper provision is made for his education and training (Section 44 CYPA 1933).

The welfare principle is of general application. It operates in all courts and whether the person concerned is a defendant or a witness. In terms of sentencing, it must be weighed alongside other—sometimes competing—considerations. This is dealt with in *Chapter 8, Sentences and Orders of the Youth Court* under *Welfare, Just Deserts and Preventing Crime.* This balancing exercise represents one of the foremost challenges for decision-makers. Other items which have their origins in the 1933 Act include:

- the separation—whenever possible—of juveniles from older offenders: p.17
- the creation of special procedures whereby juveniles facing criminal proceedings can relate to/participate in them: *Chapter 6*
- the involvement of parents or guardians in taking responsibility for their children when they become involved in the youth justice process, including attending court proceedings (and now, in various situations, being made responsible under court orders): *Chapters 6* and *8*
- the restriction of access to and reporting of youth court proceedings (with discretionary powers to extend safeguards to other courts when juveniles appear in them as defendants or witnesses) even though this principle may now be subject to inroads: see pp.48-50. As a matter of good practice, this confidentiality ought to carry over into other preliminary aspects of youth justice, failing which the later court-based restrictions will be defeated.

Further developments

The CYPA 1963 and CYPA 1969 developed this approach in various ways, including by:

- introducing special pre-court investigations and procedures, with the involvement prior to decisions about prosecution and court hearings of agencies such as social services and probation
- strengthening relevant procedures and re-affirming the special environment of the court.

Another key development was the Children Act 1989. Before the 1989 Act the then juvenile court dealt with both criminal cases *and* civil cases. The Act altered the make-up of juvenile court business by ending the court's jurisdiction in relation to civil 'care proceedings' (i.e. cases in which the authorities seek to intervene in the care or supervision of children) and similar matters. Those cases are now dealt with in the family proceedings court, leaving the youth court with an almost exclusively criminal—and thereby more focused—jurisdiction. Similarly, care orders (i.e. court orders placing children under the care of a local authority) can no longer be made—as they once could—in criminal proceedings. However, it should be noted that supervision orders to local authorities can still be made by way of sentence. Indeed, as explained in *Chapter 8,* this is an important aspect of sentencing The 1989 Act also influenced the overall picture in other ways, i.e. by:

- strengthening the concept that parents are responsible for their children and owe a specific duty to them to ensure their proper upbringing and development. Any rights which parents possess in relation to their children exist solely to assist in the furtherance of this duty

- recognising the need to support parents and all people with the care of children in the task of raising them through adolescence into adulthood. These needs were further recognised in the Crime and Disorder Act 1998 through the introduction of child safety orders and parenting orders (see *Chapter 8*)
- engendering the concept that children should be 'listened to' whenever their circumstances are under official scrutiny—on the basis that criminal behaviour may be the expression of some unmet need as much as anything else.

The Criminal Justice Act 1991

The 1991 Act is the key sentencing statute in England and Wales. Its general provisions—including the sentencing framework described in *Chapter 8*—apply to offenders of all ages. For the most part, the 1991 Act came into force in October 1992. In setting a framework within which young offenders would be dealt with it:

- altered the name of the 'juvenile court' to the 'youth court'; and
- raised the age limit for the court so as to include young people aged 17 years but not yet 18 (this new age of 'criminal majority' being made to coincide with the age of majority generally and so as to acknowledge requirements of the United Nations Convention on the Rights of the Child).

These changes were more than cosmetic. Within a context described in later chapters, they sought to recognise that the transition from childhood into adulthood can often be difficult for all concerned and that individuals accomplish this transition at different rates and ages.

The Crime and Disorder Act 1998

In 1996 an Audit Commission report, *Misspent Youth,* typified the youth justice system as inefficient and expensive whilst doing little to deal effectively with juvenile nuisance. The report concluded that the arrangements then in place failed young people who were not being guided away from offending behaviour into constructive activities—and failed victims of crime who suffered from the inconsiderate behaviour and offending of some young people. The report recommended a shift of resources from simply processing young offenders through the system towards interventions to prevent further offending behaviour. This shift was to be achieved by:

- streamlining current processes;

- dealing more effectively with known offenders;
- piloting and evaluating targeted prevention programmes; and
- ultimately, by pooling resources and effort.

Soon after the General Election of 1997, Jack Straw, Home Secretary, set up a Task Force on Youth Justice to advise him on reform of the youth justice system. Its terms of reference were :

. . . to advise Home Office Ministers on Government proposals for the development of youth justice policies and, in particular, to provide advice on taking forward an action plan as agreed by the Interdepartmental Ministerial group on Youth Justice.

A NEW PRINCIPAL AIM

The Home Secretary's Youth Justice Task Force reviewed in detail the work of the various agencies involved in dealing with young offenders. It considered that greater focus would be achieved within the system if there were to be a *single* aim to which all the agencies dealing with young people accused of offending, or known to offend, were working. As a result of this specific recommendation, section 37 Crime and Disorder Act 1998 declares that:

It shall be the principal aim of the youth justice system to prevent offending by children and young persons.

The 1998 Act gives force to this statutory aim by placing a duty on all people and bodies carrying out functions in relation to the youth justice system to have regard to it. As already indicated, courts and youth justice practitioners will now need to reconcile this new main aim with welfare considerations: see, generally, *Chapter 8.*

Further objectives
The Task Force also recommended that the principal aim should be achieved by setting the following objectives :

- the swift administration of justice so that every young person accused of breaking the law has the matter resolved without delay;
- confronting young offenders with the consequences of their offending for themselves and their family, victims and the community;
- punishment proportionate to the seriousness and persistency of the offending behaviour;
- encouraging reparation by young offenders for victims;
- reinforcing parental responsibility; and

- helping young offenders to tackle problems associated with their offending and to develop a sense of personal responsibility.

Guidance on how to achieve these objectives is contained in Home Office circulars/notes issued prior to implementation of the 1998 Act: ✋ 📖. Relevant provisions of the 1991 and 1998 Acts are noted in appropriate parts of this handbook—and particularly in *Chapter 8*.

SOME KEY FACTS ABOUT YOUTH CRIME

In the past research studies have pointed to the following conclusions:

- the peak age of offending for male offenders rose from 15 years in 1986 to 18 years in 1994
- the peak age of offending for female offenders is 15 years[1]
- 40 per cent of crime is committed by offenders under the age of 21
- over 80 per cent of known juvenile crime is committed by males
- 60 per cent of known juvenile crime is committed by a small group of about five per cent of juvenile offenders
- 70-80 per cent of juvenile offenders do not re-offend after their first offence.

Thus—in the run-in to the Criminal Justice Act 1991 (above)—it was argued that if:

- 17-year-old offenders were brought within the ambit of the juvenile court
- even greater emphasis was placed on understanding and helping them through their transition into adulthood and their offending seen against this background
- juvenile crime was—to an extent—viewed as something which most juvenile offenders would grow out of
- juvenile crime—whilst accounting for about 20 per cent of all known crime and therefore by no means insignificant—could be seen broadly as arising on the one hand from a large group of offenders who might not re-offend and on the other hand from a small group of more persistent offenders

then juvenile crime could be placed into proper perspective, resources applied more appropriately and the issue dealt with accordingly.

---

[1] More recent Home Office data puts the peak age of known offending at 18 for both males *and* females: *Criminal Statistics, England Wales, 1997*. For an extended analysis see *NACRO Youth Crime Fact Sheet*, February 1999.

A major study 'Young People and Crime' (Home Office Research Study No. 145 by John Graham and Ben Bowling, 1995), while reinforcing some of these earlier research findings, shows that others need to be revised or modified. This was a study of self-reported offending—and thus included offences which were not detected as well as those which were—among 14 to 25 year olds. It showed *inter alia* that:

- Over half the males and about one-third of the females admit that they have committed an offence at some time, but most have committed no more than one or two minor offences.
- Males are two and a half times more likely than females to have committed an offence in the previous 12 months. The proportion of male to female offenders increased with the seriousness of the offence. The *frequency* of offending among active male offenders is also substantially higher than among active female offenders.
- About three per cent of offenders account for approximately a quarter of all offences.
- White and Afro-Caribbean young people have similar rates of offending, while Asians have significantly lower rates.
- The peak age of offending was 21 for males and 16 for females (compared with 18 and 15 respectively for *detected* offences).
- The proportion of *females* committing offences declined shortly after the mid-teens.
- However, the proportion of *males* committing offences rose with age up to the age of 18 and then remained at a similar level into the mid-twenties. While some teenagers desisted from committing further crime, other young men (e.g. 30 per cent of those in their early twenties committing offences of fraud and of theft from an employer) offended for the first time as adults. Overall, however, both the *frequency* of offending and the *seriousness* of offending declined with age. Violent behaviour rose during the teenage years, then declined significantly in the twenties. Vandalism and arson were most common in the mid-teens but rare by the early twenties. On the other hand, the proportion of young males committing property offences *increased* slightly in the early twenties; but the proportion involved in such offences as shoplifting and burglary declined whereas the proportion committing less detectable crimes like fraud and theft from employers increased.
- Factors associated with an increased likelihood of offending included:
  — low parental supervision
  — a poor relationship with at least one parent
  — truancy
  — poor achievement at school

— having delinquent friends or family members
— the use of drugs; and
— heavy use of alcohol.

Although these findings might require sentencers to modify some previous assumptions (and to question e.g. whether juvenile offenders exhibiting such traits will grow out of crime without intervention) the case for special provisions for juveniles remains as strong as ever.

THE YOUTH JUSTICE PROCESS

A good deal of decision-making in relation to juvenile offenders takes place beyond the confines of the youth court. Indeed, certain cases never reach court at all whilst other youth justice agencies often deal with offenders long after court proceedings are over (e.g. by way of a community sentence, or in some instances informally). Similarly, local authorities and other youth justice practitioners are now all concerned with the much wider statutory remit of preventing crime and dealing with behaviour which might otherwise lead to offending and an appearance in court. This handbook examines this process as a whole, including the further responsibilities now cast on local authorities, the police, statutory youth offending teams (YOTs) and others. These items are considered in the remainder of *Part I*: see *Chapter 2* which looks at the respective roles and responsibilities of all *Youth Justice Agencies & Practitioners* and *Chapter 3* which deals with the new regime under which the police can issue *Reprimands and Warnings*.

Part I also looks at the statutory arrangements for the youth court, including its jurisdiction and powers—as well as the provisions whereby important decisions affecting the lives of juvenile offenders are taken by specially trained magistrates: *Chapter 4* onwards. Central to such powers and decisions are the orders made by the youth court at the sentencing stage and these are outlined in *Part II*. *Part III* contains a number of *Explanatory Charts* designed to assist understanding of the sentencing process, including a note of those cases where, for some reason, a juvenile may appear in the ordinary magistrates' court.

THE YOUTH COURT

The youth court forms a backdrop to all other aspects of the system (although it seems that YOTs are likely to emerge as the new hub of youth justice). Certain preliminary items and distinguishing features should thus be noted at this stage. Youth courts differ from adult courts because, among other things:

- there are special pre-court procedures concerning the a͟ interview, detention and charging of juveniles and the processi͟ of their cases, including a greater emphasis than there is with͟ adults on gathering information about the juvenile, both before and during any criminal proceedings: see *Chapter 2, Youth Justice Practitioners* and *Chapter 6, Procedures, Information and Evidence*
- as already indicated, parents or guardians are—wherever possible—involved in the court proceedings (see p.63) and in the processes leading to them
- there are special in-court procedures to enable juveniles to follow the proceedings and to take part more easily: *Chapter 6*
- there is a special environment in which, e.g.:
  - —magistrates who deal with cases involving young offenders are elected to a youth court panel and undergo specialist training before sitting
  - —youth court waiting areas are separated from adult areas often with designated courtrooms and separate entrances (albeit that the longstanding 'one hour' rule preventing use of courtrooms for adult purposes an hour either side of their use for youth court proceedings has been abrogated)
  - —many courts now have designated courtrooms and separate entrances which are used only for youth court purposes (and maybe also for family proceedings)
  - —access to youth court hearings is restricted to the magistrates, officials, lawyers and other *bona fide* participants (including parents or guardians) and the press: see p.48
  - —there is limited media reporting of youth court proceedings so as to generally provide anonymity for juveniles. There are also automatic restrictions on the reporting of details likely to identify any juvenile in youth court proceedings (whether as a defendant or witness). However, in relation to *offenders*, there is now a discretion to dispense with the restriction: see p.50. Other courts have analogous powers to forbid publication, albeit these are fully discretionary
  - —there is a special form of oath for all witnesses (of whatever age) who *promise* to tell the truth rather than *swear* to do so
  - —the term 'conviction' is replaced by 'finding of guilt' and 'sentence' by 'order'.[2]

---

[2] However, despite the direction in section 59 CYPA 1933 that references to 'conviction' and 'sentence' in all prior and subsequent legislation should be replaced with these alternative terms, both legislation (sic) and common usage seem to have preserved the old terminology. A later provision to replace pleas of 'guilty' and 'not guilty' by 'admissions' and 'denials' was repealed.

ower to require a juvenile or his or her parent or
to withdraw while evidence is received if this
be in the interests of the juvenile

e' factor already mentioned in this chapter affects
-making, not just concerning disposal but, e.g. the
day-to-day local authority or Probation Service
supervision (as well as court or YOT choice of supervisor)

—there is greater flexibility in terms of the location of a youth
court hearing. The court may, after a finding of guilt, e.g.
order that the case be remitted to a juvenile's local youth
court for sentence—where there may be greater scope for
devising a constructive disposal: *Chapter 8.*

—rehabilitation periods (under the Rehabilitation of Offenders
Act 1974) for most sentences are set at a lower level than for
adults: .

AGE AND HOW IT AFFECTS RESPONSIBILITY

As has been noted, the youth court deals with criminal allegations
against young people aged ten to 17 years inclusive. However, within
this age range there is an important sub-division of juveniles into:

- **CHILDREN** i.e. those aged ten to 13 years inclusive

- **YOUNG PERSONS** i.e. those aged 14 to 17 years inclusive.

Special attention must always be paid to the precise age of the defendant
and to what extent this affects, limits or controls the actions which can be
taken and the orders which may be made. In particular it should be
noted that:

- on occasions and for specific purposes the age ranges covered by
the terms 'child' and 'young person' have been altered by statutory
instrument. Despite the general definitions above, therefore, care
must be taken when applying the terms and when considering
powers or actions which may relate to each:
- whilst the categories 'child' and 'young person' determine the
main powers of the youth court, other age limits apply for
particular purposes, thus e.g.:
  —16 and 17-year-olds can be placed on probation or ordered to
  carry out certain other forms of community sentence: *Chapter 8*

—17-year-olds are treated in the same way as adults for the purposes of police interview and detention (*Chapter 2*) and court remands (*Chapter 7*)

—the age ranges which qualify young offenders for a Detention and Training Order (*Chapter 8*) vary subject to specific criteria.

Establishing age and related matters

Ascertaining a juvenile's exact age is now usually easier than it was when standards of literacy, numeracy and public record-keeping were lower. Section 99 CYPA 1933 provides that if a defendant before any court does in fact appear to be a child or young person, then the court shall make enquiry as to that person's age. The court may take into account whatever evidence is forthcoming. Thereafter, whatever the defendant's actual age, it is treated as being that presumed by the court. Neither the proceedings nor any order or judgement is invalidated if it afterwards appears that the correct age is different.

Section 48(1) of the 1933 Act also provides that the youth court may continue with and finalise proceedings against a defendant even if it appears before the end of those proceedings that the defendant is in fact 18 years of age or older. This avoids the need to refer the case to an adult court. The youth court procedures continue to operate—although other powers, especially those affecting sentencing, may need to be related to the defendant's actual age as it then appears. In this respect, section 29 CYPA 1963 allows the court a choice, in effect, in that if the defendant becomes 18 during the proceedings it may continue to deal with him or her and make any order it could have made if he or she had not become 18. As an alternative, section 47 Crime and Disorder Act 1998 provides for a youth court to remit an offender who becomes 18 during proceedings in the youth court to the adult court for the same area.

Terminology: use of the word 'juvenile' in this handbook

The word 'juvenile' is retained in this handbook to refer to young people aged ten to 17 years inclusive, even though it might appear more correct—following the change of the name of the court—to describe such people as 'youths'. However, the term 'juvenile' has survived in day-to-day use in many areas. This may be due to force of habit, or simply that this had always been the accepted way of describing someone who is not an 'adult'. As already noted, other descriptions such as 'child' or 'young person' have more specific connotations (see p.18)—whilst the term 'young offender', in its broadest sense, includes those up to 21.

Age and maturity

A significant feature of the Criminal Justice Act 1991 in creating a youth court dealing with offenders up to and including 17 years of age was the that those at the top end of the youth court age range, the 16 ar olds, would be making the transition into adulthood and oming to what was then believed to be the peak age for their ; (certainly in the case of male offenders who were thought to account for some 80 per cent of juvenile crime). Juveniles in this age group would be coping with this transition in differing ways and at differing rates of progress. They might be 'young adults'— well aware of the circumstances and consequences of their behaviour—or 'old children'—who might still be unable to cope with the responsibilities of impending adulthood. This age-related aspect is discussed in *Chapter 8*.

Age of criminal responsibility

Media attention has sometimes focused on cases where children below the age of ten have committed acts which, had they been slightly older, might well have resulted in prosecution for a serious offence. Prosecution is not possible because section 50 CYPA 1933 provides that:

> It shall be conclusively presumed that no child under the age of ten years can be guilty of an offence.

Concern has been expressed that such behaviour could well go unaddressed, especially if the child or parents concerned are not willing to respond to any form of voluntary supervision or assistance offered by agencies such as local authority social services. Suggestions have also been made that such a state of affairs can bring the criminal justice process into disrepute. Worrying though these rare occurrences are, there are no exceptions to the presumption that a child below the age of ten cannot be guilty of a crime—also known by the Latin tag *doli incapax*.

However, civil care or supervision proceedings of the kind mentioned earlier in this chapter are sometimes possible and appropriate, based not directly on any *criminal* behaviour but, e.g. on the likelihood of the child suffering significant harm. Such proceedings— under the Children Act 1989—would come before the family proceedings court from where, depending on the nature of the case, they could find their way to the county court or High Court (where making the child a ward of court might also be a possibility). Additionally, in order to safeguard the welfare of children *under ten* who may be involved in what would otherwise be criminal activity, the Crime and Disorder Act 1998 introduced child safety orders which allows a family proceedings court (NB *not* a youth court) on the application of a local authority to make an order preventing such behaviour. These orders should also be viewed in the context of child curfew orders under section 14 of the 1998 Act and parenting orders under section 8. Relevant aspects are mentioned in *Chapter 8*.

It should be noted that child safety orders and child curfew orders *only* apply to children below ten years of age. They differ altogether in kind from, e.g. anti-social behaviour orders or curfew orders following conviction of a criminal offence of a child aged ten or over: *Chapter 8.*

Children aged ten but under 14 years of age
Until 1998, the *irrebuttable* presumption that children under ten years of age were *doli incapax* (above) was treated as a *rebuttable* presumption in relation to children aged between ten and 13. In such cases, the prosecutor was required to prove:

- that the juvenile committed the *actus reus* (i.e. the physical act involved in the offence);
- that he or she had the *mens rea* (i.e. the relevant mental intent where the offence requires one); and
- that he or she *knew that what they were doing was seriously wrong* (not necessarily that he or she understood that the behaviour amounted to a criminal offence, but certainly that it was more than merely naughty).

Section 34 Crime and Disorder Act 1998 abolished this rebuttable presumption of *doli incapax* in respect of children aged between ten and 13 years in relation to anything done after 30 September 1998. As a result, *all* juveniles—i.e. those above the age of criminal responsibility—are to be treated as equals when deciding whether or not prosecution/conviction is possible.

Fourteen years and above
In the absence of some special defence (e.g. insanity), a juvenile aged 14 or over is presumed to have sufficient ability to understand the wrongness of his or her actions and to take responsibility for them. This is now the position with *all* children aged ten or over (previous heading).

Abolition of the former special rule in relation to the offence of rape
Prior to the Sexual Offences Act 1993 there was a longstanding common law presumption that a boy under the age of 14 years was physically incapable of the act of rape (or assault with intent to rape). Section 1 of the 1993 Act recognised changes over the years in the physical development of children and abolished the presumption.

OTHER DEVELOPMENTS IN YOUTH JUSTICE

Quite apart from the impact of the Crime and Disorder Act 1998 which is the main focus of this second edition of *Introduction to Youth Justice*, two further developments are worthy of note—both of which seek to remove youth offending from the formal youth court process (which leads, almost inevitably, to a system dominated by professionals and traditional outcomes which can be counter-productive).

Family group conferencing
The family group conference (FGC) seeks to capitalise on the potential of the family to resolve the problems of family members. FGCs also acknowledge that solutions arrived at and implemented by the family are likely to carry greater credence than if imposed by the state as well as offering the prospect of reintegrating adolescent offenders into the community rather than excluding them. There is also a strong emphasis on the interests of victims and associated reparation.

During the 1970s and 1980s there was increasing public alarm in New Zealand over the disproportionate number of Maori children represented on the caseloads of social workers and being accommodated in care—often with the families of white New Zealanders. A Ministerial Advisory Committee concluded that there was a need for a more culturally sensitive approach to work involving families from Maori and Pacific Island groups. The Children, Young Persons and their Families Act 1989 enshrined family group conferencing in New Zealand as the main decision-making mechanism in both welfare and youth justice based cases. The FGC is defined by that Act as a meeting convened by a co-ordinator who is responsible for ensuring, in care and protection cases, that the following functions are carried out:

- consideration of any matters relevant to the care and protection of the children concerned
- deciding whether the children are in need of care and protection
- making decisions as to the appropriate levels of care and protection; and
- reviewing the decisions and plans and their implementation.

FGCs: A United Kingdom perspective
In the UK, FGCs began as a child welfare model following interest shown at a Family Rights Group training event in 1990 after which support funding was obtained from the Department of Health for six pilot projects. What follows is based on the experiences of one of these projects, based in North-Hampshire, where the project group obtained additional funding from a number of local charities and organizations to cover implementation. Research over the life of the project showed that:

- FGCs took considerably less time than court hearings from offence to final decision

- on average about ten people attended FGCs—mainly equally split between family members and professionals
- victims of crime attended conferences in more than 50% of cases
- reparation, including a direct or indirect apology, was part of the agreed plan in over 50% of cases
- other support was offered to the young person concerned in over 66% of cases
- the majority of families felt the FGC to have had a positive effect on reducing the likelihood of the young person re-offending
- 90% of families commented positively on the experience of being involved in decision-making for family members.

The involvement of families in decision-making and the consequent need for professionals to allow this to happen is reportedly one of the most positive outcomes of the UK experiment.

Referral orders
The Youth Justice and Criminal Evidence Bill provides for the referral of young offenders to 'youth offender panels', first outlined in the White Paper *No More Excuses* (1997). The Bill is likely to receive Royal Assent during 1999 and referral orders to be piloted from April 2000 onwards.

The idea is that this order will become the standard sentence imposed by the youth court for first time juvenile offenders. The proposed order will be a sentence of the court (but not a community sentence: see *Chapter 8*), will not require a pre-sentence report (PSR) and will run for between three months and a year. Parents, guardians or some other 'appropriate person' could also be ordered to participate in the order by attending meetings. Victims might also attend as well as anyone over 18 who appears capable exerting some positive influence on the juvenile. Most other orders of the youth court would be prohibited if a referral order is made.

It is intended that YOTs will be responsible for implementation of such referral orders which will involve attendance at meetings of a youth offender panel made up of YOT members and other people specially appointed to deal with individual offenders. An early aim of the youth offending panel will be to forge an agreement with the offender on a programme designed to prevent offending. If the referral fails for any reason, the matter would be sent back to court—with the possibility that the offender could be re-sentenced for the original offence. It must be stressed that these proposals are currently still in embryo: 📖✍

CHAPTER 2

Youth Justice Agencies & Practitioners

As indicated in *Chapter 1*, the youth justice process involves a variety of responsibilities and decision-makers in addressing issues concerning juvenile offenders as they make their transition into adulthood.

A MULTI-AGENCY APPROACH

It has long been seen as appropriate/desirable to invest time, energies, resources and understanding to deal with this age group, e.g. to:

- prevent offending by children and young persons
- make positive interventions at an early stage
- provide constructive outlets for youthful energies
- try to protect those who do offend from their own behaviour and to help them through what can be a difficult time in their lives and individual development
- provide positive interventions at an early stage of criminal behaviour
- provide disposals and orders on their being found guilty by a court which address offending behaviour and help them to prepare for adulthood.

In pursuit of these aims and in balancing the just deserts approach with the welfare principle and preventing offences (*Chapter 8*) it is essential that all agencies having dealings with people in this age group, whether immediately within the youth justice process or on a wider basis, adopt co-ordinated and integrated procedures and strategies to maximise resources and avoid conflicting actions.

As emphasised in *Chapter 1*, the Crime and Disorder Act 1998 requires all agencies to have regard to the principal statutory aim of the youth justice system which is *to prevent offending by children and young persons*—and a duty is placed on all people and bodies carrying out functions in relation to youth justice to have regard to this aim. It is important therefore to recognise that cooperation between all the agencies—the multi-agency approach—is a prerequisite to achieving it.

The rest of this chapter outlines ways in which the various practitioners and agencies act and interact, mentioning the roles of the:

- Youth Justice Board for England and Wales
- local authorities

- youth offending teams (known as YOTs)
- social services and the Probation Service (inside or outside YOTs)
- the police
- the Crown Prosecution Service (CPS)
- solicitors (including duty solicitors)
- voluntary agencies
- members/officials of the youth court (the constitution, jurisdiction and powers of this court are considered from *Chapter 4* onwards).

THE YOUTH JUSTICE BOARD

In order to ensure that adequate structures were in place to deliver youth justice services more effectively, the government, in November 1997, announced its intention to set up a Youth Justice Board for England and Wales (*No More Excuses: A New Approach to Tackling Youth Crime in England and Wales*, Home Office/HMSO, Cm. 3809).

The purpose of the Board was seen as monitoring the delivery of youth justice services and helping to raise standards. The Board would be a non-departmental public body sponsored by the Home Office with clear and extensive functions across youth justice. Section 41 Crime and Disorder Act 1998 established the Board as a body corporate with effect from 1 October 1998. The functions of the Board were specified as:

- monitoring the operation of the youth justice system and the provision of youth justice services
- advising the Secretary of State on the operation o f the system especially with regard to how the principal statutory aim (preventing offending: above) could be achieved
- monitoring the extent to which that aim is being achieved and any set standards met
- obtaining information from relevant authorities
- publishing information
- promoting good practice
- commissioning research into good practice; and
- awarding grants to develop good practice.

As well as setting the strategic direction for the youth justice system, the Youth Justice Board will become the budget holder for all young offender secure facilities (i.e. those provided by local authorities, secure accommodation provided for detention and training orders (*Chapter 8*), secure training centres (*Chapter 8*) and the Department of Health's youth treatment centre at Glenthorne). By acting as a national budget holder for *all* secure facilities for young offenders, the Board will be in a position to ensure more cost effective regimes from providers and this will enable resources, eventually, to be shifted between custodial and non-custodial preventative interventions.

The Board will *not*, directly, manage any part of the youth justice system. It will however administer a development fund which will allow it to identify and resource local development projects on behalf of ministers and to evaluate programme effectiveness in order to prevent different areas of the country 're-inventing the wheel'.

ROLE OF THE LOCAL AUTHORITY

Whilst the Youth Justice Board will monitor the operation of the system *nationally*, the prime duty for ensuring the availability of appropriate youth justice services *in an area* lies with those local authorities with social services and education responsibilities. Section 38 Crime and Disorder Act 1998 imposes this statutory duty and further requires every chief officer of police or police authority and every probation committee or health authority in any part of the relevant local authority area to co-operate with the local authority in discharging its statutory duties. Crime prevention responsibilities are cast on all tiers of local authorities.

Funding for youth justice services in an area is to be provided by the local authority and other relevant bodies either directly or by contributing to a fund established and maintained by the authority. The statutory services required of the authority are:

- providing appropriate adults to safeguard the interests of children and young people detained or questioned by police officers
- the assessment of young people and provision of rehabilitation programmes for them
- supporting young people remanded or committed on bail while awaiting trial or sentence
- placement in local authority accommodation of those remanded or committed to such accommodation
- provision of court reports in criminal proceedings
- provision of people to act as responsible officers in relation to reparation orders and action plan orders (*Chapter 8*)
- making appropriate applications to a court for anti-social behaviour orders in respect of children over ten, and child safety orders and child curfew orders in respect of children under ten
- supervision of juveniles sentenced to supervision etc. within a youth offending team (YOT), i.e. shared responsibilities (*Chapter 8*)
- supervision of young persons sentenced to a detention and training order (*Chapter 8*)
- post-release supervision of children sentenced to custody; and
- establishing one or more YOTs for the area.

A youth justice plan

Section 40 of the 1998 Act also requires local authorities with social services and education responsibilities to formulate and implement an annual youth justice plan. This is to be done after consultation with every chief officer of police, police authority, probation committee, health authority and, where there are two tiers of local government, each district council in the area.

The youth justice plan will set out how youth justice services in the area are to be provided and funded, how the YOTs are to be composed and funded, how they are to operate and what functions they are to carry out. Annual plans will be submitted to the Youth Justice Board for approval.

YOUTH OFFENDING TEAMS (YOTs)

Section 39 Crime and Disorder Act 1998 places a duty on local authorities with social services and education responsibilities to establish one or more YOTs for their area. Chief officers of police, probation committees and health authorities are required to co-operate with the local authority in establishing such teams.

There is scope for two or more local authorities to act together to establish one or more YOTs for both or all their areas where this is considered appropriate.

Expenditure incurred by, or for purposes connected with YOTs will be met by local authorities and their statutory partner agencies either directly or from a joint fund contributed to by all agencies.

Membership of YOTs

YOTs will include at least one of each of the following:

- a probation officer
- a social worker of a local authority social services department
- a police officer
- someone nominated by a health authority in the area
- someone nominated by the chief education officer for the area.

In addition, a YOT may also include such other people as the authority thinks appropriate—thus giving scope for the involvement of and participation by voluntary agencies, local or national.

Duties of YOTs

The duties of YOTs will be:

- to co-ordinate the provision of youth justice services for those in the area who need them; and
- to carry out the functions assigned to the team in the Youth Justice Plan (above).

Strategic overview and direction of a YOT will be provided by a management team consisting of chief officers from all the main agencies involved. Day-to-day management of the team's activities will be provided by a local manager whose primary task will be to weld together the individuals from different backgrounds who make up the YOT. Most staff are likely to come on secondment from the participating agencies for either short or longer terms. They will bring with them the contractual terms and conditions of their employing agency and a diversity of working cultures.

The roles of individuals within the YOT are important—successful teams will be able to undertake duties normally associated with individual agencies. The expectation is, however, that staff bring skills with them to the team which may then be undertaken by all members or just individuals. Thus, e.g. *social workers* and *probation officers* might, subject to the local authority Youth Justice Plan, directly or indirectly:

- assess and manage risk of re-offending
- make assessments and provide interventions
- provide bail information and support services
- prepare pre-sentence and other court reports
- supervise community sentences and reparation orders
- provide through-care for young people serving custodial sentence
- deal with rehabilitation of juveniles subject to police warnings; and
- deal with parents of juvenile offenders under parenting orders.

Police officers involved with the YOT might:

- work with young offenders to highlight the effect of offending on victims and the impact of a criminal record
- organize reparation work with offenders and victims
- oversee curfew elements of bail conditions and other court orders
- liaise with colleagues running attendance centres; and
- link the work of the YOT to wider crime reduction initiatives.

Education staff might:

- help excluded children get back into school
- provide school reports to the courts
- make arrangements to meet the literacy, numeracy and other educational or training needs of young offenders; and
- provide careers advice or help in finding employment.

Health staff might:

- identify the physical and mental health needs of young offenders
- liaise with health professionals providing health care services; and
- provide advice on healthy lifestyles or drug and alcohol issues as part of work under offending behaviour programmes.

In order to test the ability of local authorities to successfully implement and manage YOTs, four pilot schemes were set up from 1 October 1998 for a period of 18 months prior to full implementation of the provisions. The pilot areas were:

- Hampshire, Portsmouth, Southampton and Isle of Wight (jointly)
- The London Boroughs of Hammersmith and Fulham, Kensington and Chelsea, City of Westminster
- Wolverhampton
- Sheffield.

POLICE RESPONSIBILITIES

In addition to their YOT involvement, the police service, as the agency investigating and prosecuting crime, has a front-line responsibility—and opportunity—to set the tone in ensuring that juveniles are treated in a manner appropriate to their ages, needs and understanding. The police act in accordance with a variety of legal requirements, including the Children and Young Persons Acts of 1933, 1963 and 1969 and the Police and Criminal Evidence Act 1984 (PACE)—and associated Codes of Practice (which govern the investigation of crime and treatment of suspects)—and the Crime and Disorder Act 1998.

It should again be noted that people aged 17 years are treated while in police detention as if they were *adults* rather than as *juveniles*. (The same is so in relation to police or court decisions about bail or custody: *Chapter 7*).

Some specific police functions

Many police functions under PACE fall to be discharged by a custody officer (usually a police sergeant who has been given the duty to ensure the operation of statutory and other safeguards for people detained in police custody). These include:

- if a detained person appears to be under 17 years of age, treating that person as if he or she were of that age in the absence of clear evidence to the contrary

- separating detained juveniles from other people in police detention (with female juveniles being under the care of a woman) (Section 31 CYPA 1933)
- taking such immediate steps as are practicable to ascertain who is responsible for a detained juvenile's welfare (i.e. parent, guardian, local authority if the juvenile is in care, or any other person who has assumed such responsibility) and to inform that person about the juvenile's arrest, the reason for it and the reason for any continued detention (Section 34(2) CYPA 1933)
- where the juvenile is already subject to a supervision order (made in criminal or civil proceedings), notifying the appropriate supervisor /YOT (Section 34(7) CYPA 1933)
- notifying the relevant local authority where the detained juvenile is being provided with accommodation by that authority under the Children Act 1989
- in any event, allowing a detained juvenile to exercise the general right under section 56 of PACE to have a friend, relative or other interested person informed about the fact of his or her detention
- arranging for the removal of a detained juvenile to local authority accommodation unless certain exceptions apply
- making arrangements for access to legal advice if so requested
- ensuring that any interview takes place in the presence of an 'appropriate adult' (i.e. parent, guardian, representative of a relevant local authority or voluntary organization where the juvenile is in care, his or her youth worker or any responsible person aged 18 years or more who is not a police officer or police employee: YOTs can provide appropriate adults). The appropriate adult's function is to advise the juvenile, facilitate communication with him or her and observe whether the interview is conducted properly and fairly.
- considering whether to give a reprimand or final warning rather than prosecute: see *Chapter 3;* and
- ensuring that the detained juvenile is granted bail if and as appropriate: see generally *Chapter 7.*

Broader police activities concerning juveniles
However, the special role of the police in youth justice matters should not be viewed exclusively from the standpoint of investigative and interviewing processes. Police forces adopt a broad approach to such matters, including:

- involvement as full-time members of YOTs
- involvement in crime prevention and crime reduction initiatives, e.g. contributing to projects, giving talks to youth groups, schools

- involvement in offender discussion groups particularly when arranged under a supervision order or probation order; and
- allowing individual police officers in their own time to run or assist at attendance centres (see *Chapter 8*) where they and offenders can, as in offender discussion groups, interact outside the usual police processes.

CROWN PROSECUTION SERVICE

Just as the police have a role to play in ensuring the proper handling of juvenile offenders so does the Crown Prosecution Service (CPS) which is responsible for taking over the great majority of police prosecutions following a decision to bring court proceedings. This includes:

- as part of an initial and continuing duty, to review cases brought by the police against juveniles (and in certain cases those brought by other people as well) and to see whether a reprimand or final warning (*Chapter 3*) might yet be appropriate, despite the fact that formal proceedings have been begun
- being aware of and acting within the special procedures and considerations applicable to juvenile offenders, e.g. as outlined in *Chapter 1* of this handbook and in the CPS's own Code (below)
- being prepared in presenting the facts of a case against a juvenile to provide available information which might help in balancing the just deserts approach with the welfare principle and the need to prevent offending: *Chapter 8*
- being especially attentive to the Police and Criminal Evidence Act 1984 (PACE) and the PACE Codes as they apply to juveniles.

Further, in considering whether or not to prosecute, the Crown prosecutor must apply two tests: an 'evidential test' (i.e. broadly speaking, 'Is there a reasonable prospect of a conviction?') and a 'public interest test' (i.e. 'Does the public interest warrant proceedings being brought or continued with?'). In relation to juveniles, there are special requirements in the Code for Crown Prosecutors as follows:

Code requirements re youth offenders
Crown prosecutors must consider the interests of a youth when deciding whether it is in the public interest to prosecute; the stigma of a conviction can cause very serious harm to the prospects of a youth offender; young offenders can sometimes be dealt with without going to court; but Crown prosecutors should not avoid prosecuting simply because of the defendant's age. The seriousness of the offence or the offender's past behaviour may make prosecution necessary.

Requirements re police warnings and reprimands
Similarly the CPS Code acknowledges that the police make the decision
to reprimand or warn an offender in accordance with Home Office
guidelines and that if the defendant admits the offence, reprimand or
warning is, subject to those guidelines, the most common alternative to a
court appearance. Crown prosecutors, where necessary, apply the same
guidelines and should look at the alternatives to prosecution when they
consider the public interest. They should tell the police if they think that
a reprimand or warning would be more suitable than prosecution. See
also *Chapter 3, Reprimands and Warnings.*

DEFENCE SOLICITORS

Although this handbook cannot examine in detail the role of the solicitor
or other advocate in relation to procedures concerning juveniles at the
police station or court, it is clear that such practitioners (including court
duty solicitors) have their part to play in helping to establish the special
environment relating to juvenile offenders. In particular they can:

- be aware of and sensitive to the provisions noted above relating to
  police detention and the questioning of juvenile offenders
- interact appropriately at all stages with the juvenile, parents,
  appropriate adults, YOTS and individual statutory agencies
- understand the relatively complex bail/custody provisions which
  apply to juveniles (*Chapter 7*) and assist in ensuring their proper
  consideration and application
- understand the special environment, procedures and powers in the
  youth court and be ready to act within them
- understand the system for reprimands and final warnings (*Chapter
  3*) and be prepared to advocate such a course when appropriate.

SOCIAL SERVICES/PROBATION

In addition to the duties and responsibilities imposed by the Crime and
Disorder Act 1998 (above), there is a statutory duty on Probation
Services[1] and Social Services Departments to respond to the initiation of
proceedings by a prosecutor:

> It shall be the duty of a person who decides to lay an information in respect
> of an offence in a case where he has reason to believe that the alleged

---

[1]   For a fuller explanation of the role of the Probation Service in relation to the
youth court see *Introduction to the Probation Service,* Dick Whitfield, Waterside
Press 1998, particularly *Chapter 8.*

offender is a young person[2] to give notice of the decision to the appropriate local authority[3] unless he is himself that authority. (Section 5(8) Children and Young Persons Act 1969)

Section 9 of the 1969 Act requires the local authority, on receipt of such notice, unless it considers it to be 'unnecessary', to investigate and report to the court on the juvenile's home surroundings, school record, health and character. Strictly speaking, this provision is separate from the pre-sentence report (PSR) considerations which arise following a finding of guilt (see *Chapter 6*)—although, by local agreement, such investigation and reporting is often left until the PSR stage. This would not preclude the local authority from making an interim report at any stage where there are known factors worthy of the court's immediate attention. The court can always require such an initial report if it is thought necessary.

In addition to their involvement with YOTs, Probation Services may become involved in the provision of youth justice services in other ways:

- whilst not funded to provide accommodation in a similar way to social services, the probation service will, in appropriate circumstances, provide a place in a bail hostel for juveniles aged 16 and 17 years who are on bail granted by a court (a police officer cannot impose such a condition when granting bail). Funding difficulties can arise in respect of juvenile placements. It should be noted in this respect that a bail placement for a 16 year old in a probation hostel requires the prior authority of the Secretary of State (see Home Office Circular 46/1993). Equally, the probation service may offer a place in a probation hostel for those 16 and 17 year olds subject to a probation order (but not a supervision order) with such a requirement. However, such placement should be approved by an assistant chief probation officer with special responsibility for such decisions (again, see HOC 46/1993). All people in a hostel are expected to contribute according to their means.
- outside of operating probation orders, community service orders and combination orders, the service has no direct overall statutory responsibility (as local authorities do: above)
- the service involves itself in crime prevention and reduction initiatives in accordance with a Home Office three-year plan (currently for 1996-1999) and pursuant to the 1998 Act—although its main statutory responsibility relates to the supervision of court orders.

---

[2] NB: in this case the term young person covers the full ten to 17 years age range.
[3] Usually the authority where the young person resides

The probation equivalent to section 5(8) and section 9 Children and Young Persons Act 1969 (above) is contained in section 34(2) of that Act:

> In the case of a person who has not attained the age of eighteen but has attained such lower age as the Secretary of State may by order specify no proceedings for an offence shall be begun in any court unless the person proposing to begin the proceedings has, in addition to any notice falling to be given by him to a local authority in pursuance of section 5(8) of this Act, given notice of the proceedings to a probation officer for the area for which the court acts.

VOLUNTARY ORGANIZATIONS

Many voluntary organizations are active in youth work, often with a view to providing activities aimed at helping young people within the age range covered by the youth court to find meaningful outlets through which their overall development can be aided. In many cases the issue of offending will also be addressed in general terms. A representative of a voluntary agency can become part of a YOT.

In 1983 the then Department of Health and Social Security made significant sums of money available in England and Wales to voluntary organizations working in collaboration with local authorities and often in a multi-agency setting with other interested parties (e.g. the police, probation service and even, in an indirect or purely advisory capacity, the magistracy), to develop local community based schemes which could be used to address juvenile offending, particularly through supervision orders with special requirements. The tradition established by these early partnerships, including their crime prevention role, continues.[4]

YOUTH COURTS AS PART OF THIS PROCESS

It might seem that youth courts (*Chapter 1* and *Chapter 4* onwards) are in the main merely recipients of the results of the activities of other youth justices practitioners. This would possibly be so if the youth justice system was to be seen in linear terms with the court being just one stage in the process from offending, through investigation, detection, prosecution, trial and—given a properly obtained conviction—disposal by way of sentence (*Chapter 8*). If youth justice, however, is seen in global and more 'interactive' terms the youth court is ideally placed to foster an integrated approach. This has been the traditional stance in many areas

---

[4] *The ISTD Handbook of Community Programmes* compiled and edited by Carol Martin contains a wide range of examples, including many programmes for juveniles (Waterside Press/ISTD, 1998)

of the country where courts have encouraged initiatives by practitioners and been prepared to use sometimes quite progressive local schemes.

A central position
Given its central role, the youth court has always been in a good position to enhanced the efforts of others in the process by, e.g.

- summoning parents or guardians to court and ensuring their attendance and full participation in the hearing and, where appropriate, the operation of any subsequent order
- leading by example by ensuring that the special environment in court is established and maintained
- being prepared to convene multi-agency groups (such as court user groups) or to play its part in any wider liaison arrangements.

Magistrates must always maintain a judicial stance. They can, however, be proactive to the benefit of youth justice as a whole: in future, e.g. supporting the work of YOTs, potentially the new hub of youth justice.

The justices' clerk
The role of the justices' clerk vis-à-vis the youth court encompasses his or her duties as legal adviser (*Chapter 4*) plus a liaison responsibility in relation to the agencies already mentioned (possibly in conjunction with the justices' chief executive for the area). It is centrally important that all court legal staff understand the policies and strategies of other agencies and keep youth panel magistrates informed of schemes and developments—which affect their ability to make appropriate decisions.

SECTION 95 CRIMINAL JUSTICE ACT 1991

All practitioners should note section 95 of the 1991 Act which places a duty on the Home Secretary to inform sentencers and other people engaged in the administration of justice about the financial implications of their decisions and to publish information about matters such as race and gender. In the latter context, the statutory purpose is expressed as being to facilitate the performance of such people of

> their duty to avoid discriminating against any person on the ground of race, sex or any other improper ground.

The most recent Home Office publications are available locally, e.g. through clerks to justices, chief probation officers, etc. ✺ ▢. Courts have made considerable efforts to improve their understanding of race, ethnic, gender and other minority issues, and this is something which other agencies can assist with through their own day-to-day practices.

CHAPTER 3

Reprimands and Warnings

The non-statutory practice of the police cautioning a juvenile offender rather than prosecuting began as an informal response to many of the issues discussed in *Chapter 1*.

BACKGROUND

Home Office Circular 14/1985 gave the existing practice of cautioning a national impetus and further direction was contained in Home Office Circular 18/1994. The thinking behind the practice—particularly in respect of juveniles—was that if offenders would admit their offending and face up to it in some form of controlled, but out of court, situation then there was no need to invoke the full weight of the youth justice process, or to stigmatise the offender with a criminal record. Some research studies showed that up to 80 per cent of first-time juvenile offenders ceased to offend after their behaviour came to official attention. Juveniles and their parents would therefore hopefully respond positively to this 'shot across the bows' and the juvenile would then use the experience in adopting a more responsible approach whilst growing up.

So much store was set by cautioning, that in 1994 some 87 per cent of males and 97 per cent of females in the ten to 13 years age range (i.e. 'children': see *Chapter 1*) were cautioned rather than prosecuted for indictable offences.

When fully implemented, the Crime and Disorder Act 1998 will replace the informal cautioning system with a statutory scheme encompassing *reprimands* and final *warnings*. The informal scheme was seen as too inconsistent and providing little, nationally, in the way of effective interventions. The aim of the new scheme is to make it clear to young offenders that there is an immediate cut-off point for offending behaviour, after which a prosecution in the youth court will be instigated.

CRIME AND DISORDER ACT 1998

The new scheme is referred to in the relevant literature as the 'Final Warning Scheme', which incorporates both the reprimand and the warning. That label is something of a misnomer because—as described below—an offender can receive a reprimand and two warnings in certain circumstances before he or she is prosecuted.

Although the new scheme operates as an alternative to prosecution, it remains open to the police to prosecute in each and every case.

'Reprimands' and 'warnings'

A *reprimand* can be viewed as the equivalent of a police caution under the old system; a *warning* as a version of what became known as 'caution plus', i.e. a caution followed by some form of intervention designed to address offending behaviour. In future, intervention, probably more structured/sophisticated, will be supervised by the YOT.

Both of the new options are aimed at preventing an offender from re-offending. However, the Final Warning Scheme (see next section) should not be viewed as an easy option. Offenders will have to participate in a YOT rehabilitation programme if they have been given a warning; and additionally, future courts are restricted as to sentence so that a conditional discharge (*Chapter 8*) may only be given in certain circumstances if a defendant has previously received a warning. The intention is that young offenders will come to appreciate that if they do not amend their behaviour after a reprimand or warning any further appearance before a court will result in significant punishment.

Designed to be quick and effective

In this way the new scheme links in with the principal statutory aim of preventing offending by children and young people. In particular, it addresses the problems caused by repeat offending by ensuring that offending behaviour is addressed quickly outside the court arena, and— if this does not work—that offenders are brought before the court quickly and dealt with effectively.

A matter for the police

The decision as to the most appropriate action to take, i.e. whether to issue a reprimand, warning, or to prosecute remains with the police. They are not obliged to discuss the case with any other agency and whether they do so will be a matter for local practice. Multi-agency 'gatekeeping' (the former system whereby different agencies might have a more or less equal input at this early stage) no longer applies.

THE NEW 'FINAL WARNING SCHEME'

The effect of section 65 Crime and Disorder Act 1998 is that a reprimand or warning can only be given in the following circumstances, i.e. where:

- a constable has evidence that a child or young person ('the offender') has committed an offence

- the constable considers that the evidence is such that, if the offender were to be prosecuted for the offence, there would be a realistic prospect of a conviction
- the offender admits to the constable that he or she committed the offence
- the offender has not previously been convicted of an offence; and
- the constable is satisfied that it would not be in the public interest for the offender to be prosecuted.

The public interest test used by the police in deciding whether or not to issue a reprimand or warning is similar to that used by the Crown prosecutor in deciding whether or not to prosecute (see p.31).

Restrictions on repeat reprimands or warnings
There are limits on the number of times an offender can be given a reprimand or warning as follows:

Reprimands
A reprimand may only be given if the offender has not previously been reprimanded or warned (i.e. only for a first offence).

Warnings
A warning may be given instead of a reprimand for the offender's first offence if the constable considers that offence to be so serious as to require a warning. However, usually a reprimand is given for a first offence and a warning can only be given for such a first offence if the seriousness of the offence requires it. If the offence is only sufficiently serious for a reprimand, the police officer should not issue a warning in order to ensure that a rehabilitation programme is instigated. Instead, if the officer feels that intervention is necessary, information about appropriate voluntary agencies should be given to the offender. Otherwise a constable may issue a warning to the offender if:

- the offender has not previously been warned (i.e. for a first offence, or for a second offence having been given a reprimand for the first offence); or
- the offender has previously been warned and the offence was committed more than two years after the date of that previous warning *and* the constable considers the offence to be not so serious as to require a prosecution to be brought (i.e. for a second or third offence as the case may be).

When deciding whether or not to prosecute (often called 'charge' at this stage) or to administer a second warning, there is presumption in favour of prosecuting the juvenile for the alleged offence.

Transitional arrangements
In making the decision whether or not to issue a reprimand or warning:

- any caution given to a child or young person before the Final Warning Scheme came into effect must be treated as if it were a reprimand; and
- any offender who has received a second or subsequent caution must be deemed to have been given a warning.

ROLE OF THE POLICE

As indicated under the heading *A matter for the police*, the question whether to administer a reprimand, warning or to prosecute is solely for the police without consultation with any other agency. The decision should be made soon after arrest and the offender should be brought to court immediately where appropriate.

Draft guidance to the police states that the Final Warning Scheme should never be used for the most serious indictable only offences, e.g. rape and murder; and only in other purely indictable cases in exceptional circumstances. Thus, e.g. either way offences such as theft, criminal damage, assault and burglary *are* within the ambit of a reprimand or warning.

The advice makes it clear that an admission of an offence must not be obtained by holding out the option of a reprimand or warning instead of prosecuting the juvenile.

Involvement of parents and guardians
Encouragement is given to parents or guardians to attend when a warning is given to persuade them to accept their responsibility for their child's behaviour. There is no *statutory* requirement for a 17 year old offender's parent or guardian to attend the police station although this may be desirable in most cases. An appropriate adult must be present during the administering of a warning or reprimand to an offender aged under 16. Such a person is entitled to a copy of any documentation.

The formalities
Both the reprimand and the warning must be given orally but should be recorded as soon as possible after being administered. A police officer issuing a reprimand or warning must be in uniform and will usually be of the rank of inspector or above.

Reprimand
When giving a reprimand the officer must state:

- the details of the offence or offences which have resulted in the arrest
- that in all but exceptional circumstances any further offending will result in a warning or prosecution
- that for a recordable offence, a reprimand constitutes a criminal record for employment purposes; and
- that for all offences, the fact that a defendant has been given a reprimand can be placed before a court in future proceedings.

Warning
When giving a warning, the officer must specify:

- the details of the offence/offences which have resulted in the warning
- that the warning is a serious matter
- that further offending will usually result in charges being brought
- that for any recordable offences, the warning constitutes a criminal record for employment purposes
- that the warning may be cited in any future criminal proceedings
- that if the offender is convicted of a further offence within two years it is unlikely, save in exceptional circumstances, that a conditional discharge will be available to the court as a sentencing option (see p.43)
- that the offender will be referred immediately to a YOT for assessment and participation in a rehabilitation programme
- that a report will be written if the offender fails to comply unreasonably with the rehabilitation programme and may be cited in any future court proceedings; and
- details of the YOT and where further information can be obtained.

It is envisaged that the police will pass on to the YOT daily the details of offenders who have been given a warning along with any additional information they feel would be relevant to any assessment.

ROLE OF THE YOUTH OFFENDING TEAM

As already indicated, when a constable gives an offender a warning he or she must refer that offender to a YOT. The YOT is then under an obligation to assess the offender and arrange for him or her to participate in a rehabilitation programme, unless it is considered inappropriate to do so. A member of the YOT must:

- contact the offender within two working days
- arrange an initial assessment meeting as soon as possible; and

- assess the offender to determine whether a rehabilitation programme is appropriate and, if one is, identify the key issues that the programme should address.

Assessment
The assessment should take into account:

- the reasons for the offending
- the circumstances of the offence
- the effect on the victim
- the support networks available to the offender; and
- whether friends and family of the victim are willing to become involved in the rehabilitation programme.

If a programme is not considered appropriate, the offender and his parents/guardian and the police must be notified in writing giving the reasons why that decision has been made.

The rehabilitation programme
Government guidance to YOTs states that a member of staff will be allocated to the offender once notified that an offender has been referred by the police following the warning. The programme must be aimed at rehabilitating the offender and preventing him or her from re-offending. Therefore, any rehabilitation programme must be detailed, and be drawn up in conjunction with the offender, his or her parents or guardians, and anyone else considered appropriate. It must have achievable timescales. The programme's aims must be:

- clear
- reasonable
- agreed in advance
- commensurate with the seriousness of the offence
- achievable in terms of time; and
- recorded (with a copy given to the offender and his or her parents or guardians).

Each programme is individual to the offender but will always be targeted at achieving the overall aims of addressing offending behaviour and preventing re-offending. Research from various pre-1998 Act 'caution plus' schemes (p.36) suggests that there are a number of factors common to youth offending which need to be addressed. These include:

- a troubled home life
- education problems
- deprivation

- peer pressure
- personal issues.

The research showed that these problems often manifested themselves in the following behaviours:

- emotional (e.g. frustration)
- physical (e.g. hyperactivity)
- anti-social (e.g. bullying)
- substance misuse
- criminality.

These areas can be addressed by any of the agencies that form part of the local YOT.

Victims and reparation

If a warning is issued, any victim must be notified. Usually the associated programme should include reparation to the victim and/or the community. It is envisaged that this could take a variety of forms, from an apology to the victim to some form of community activity. In all cases, the victim must be consulted. Reparation could be any or all of the following:

- apology to the victim, oral, written or by video
- voluntary financial compensation
- compensation in kind (e.g. gardening)
- donation to charity
- community activity.

The final decision about the content of the programme and any form of reparation is that of the YOT only, although the demands made on the offender should not be too onerous having regard to the nature of the offence and the effect on the victim. The victim must be consulted about the suggested form of reparation. If there is to be any face-to-face meeting care needs to be taken that the victim is comfortable with this, has been consulted in advance, and that sufficient protection is given at the meeting (to both parties).

Other elements of the programme

These can include:

- counselling
- education and skills development
- medical interventions to deal with physical or mental issues
- building parenting skills.

Other actions not forming part of the programme but which may supplement it are:

- tackling areas such as housing needs/claiming the correct benefits
- reference to a mentoring scheme.

Non-compliance by the offender

If an offender does not comply with the programme and there are valid reasons for not doing so (e.g. illness), the YOT can re-assess the programme. However, if there are no valid reasons, the YOT must write to the offender and his or her parents/guardians notifying them that if he or she does not comply this will be noted and placed before the court in any future proceedings. If necessary the programme can be modified at that stage. Any further non-compliance should be noted and details sent to the offender, his or her parents/guardian, and the police.

REPRIMANDS, WARNINGS AND THE COURT

The youth court is affected by reprimands and warnings via:

- a statutory restriction on its sentencing powers
- information on a defendant's record of previous convictions.

Sentencing restrictions

Where someone commits an offence *within two years* of receiving a warning, the sentencing court may not make an order for conditional discharge unless of opinion that there are exceptional circumstances relating to the offence or the offender. If the court does order a conditional discharge it must state in open court that it is of this opinion and say why. These reasons are recorded in the court register. Two *cautions* do not equate with a warning for the purpose of barring a conditional discharge, however. The fact that a defendant has received two cautions in the past (i.e. under the pre-1998 Act arrangements), whilst it prevents a warning being given, does not preclude the court from making an order for conditional discharge. There is no restriction on a court giving an *absolute* discharge if appropriate.

Information to courts

If a defendant is convicted of an offence, the following information will be before the court in the same way as that about previous convictions:

- that the defendant has been given a reprimand previously; and/or
- that the defendant has been given a warning previously; and
- any report prepared as a result of the defendant failing to participate in a rehabilitation programme arranged after a warning.

CHAPTER 4

The Youth Court: (1) Constitution

As outlined in *Chapter 1*, the youth court replaced the juvenile court and came into being when the main provisions of the Criminal Justice Act 1991 were implemented in October 1992. It operates through a youth court panel under the general auspices of the local magistrates' court.

THE YOUTH COURT PANEL

Each petty sessions area must maintain a youth court panel. The magistrates for the area, at their annual election meeting (their 'October meeting') must, every third year, appoint such a panel. The magistrates so appointed are required to be 'specially qualified for dealing with juvenile cases'. Special arrangements exist for Inner London.

The number of members appointed must be such as the magistrates on the particular bench think sufficient to deal with youth court business (bearing in mind also that the Lord Chancellor expects 13 youth court sittings a year as a minimum). They may, at any time, appoint additional members. If additional appointees cannot be found from the petty sessions area concerned then members may, if necessary, be appointed from other areas in the same commission area. Magistrates can be appointed to the panel up to age 70. It was formerly recommended (before youth courts replaced juvenile courts and when the age limit was 65), that there be no first time appointment to the panel over age 50.

At the time of writing, the present panels were appointed in October 1997 and cease to exist on the 31 December 2000. Hence, the next appointments will take place at annual meetings of benches held in October 2000, and every third year after that. Vacancies in the membership of a panel must be filled as soon as practicable, unless this is considered not to be necessary. A magistrate appointed to fill a vacancy, or as an additional member, serves until the end of the period for which the other members of the panel were originally appointed.

A stipendiary magistrate is, by virtue of his or her office, a member of the youth court panel for the petty sessions area where he or she exercises jurisdiction.

A local magistrates' courts committee (the body responsible for the provision of the court service in a given area of the country) may make recommendations to the Lord Chancellor: (a) for the formation of a combined youth court panel for two or more petty sessions areas; or (b) for the dissolution of any such combined youth court panel, provided that the committee's area comprises at least one of the petty sessions areas concerned. In practice, many panels, particularly in rural areas, are 'combined' panels.

TRAINING FOR THE YOUTH COURT PANEL

A magistrate, on becoming a member of a youth court panel, is required to undertake a course of instruction to be completed within a year of appointment. The instruction is carried out in stages and intended to enable the magistrate to gain a full understanding of the place of the youth court in the judicial system, and the principles and procedures applicable in such courts. In addition, it is intended that magistrates should gain an understanding of juveniles appearing before the court and a knowledge of the services and orders which are available. The training is divided as follows:

- the Foundation Programme
- the Basic Programme; and
- Refresher Training.

What is described below represents only an outline syllabus, which is expected to be implemented in a flexible manner to meet local and regional circumstances.

Foundation programme
The Foundation Programme, which has to be carried out before the magistrate first sits in the youth court, consists of three parts. The first part requires the magistrate to attend a sitting of the youth court as an observer. The second part of the programme comprises information about the background of young offenders, and practices and procedures relating to the youth court, together with detailed information about remands, trials, pre-sentence reports and sentencing. Finally, before sitting in the youth court to hear actual cases, a magistrate should attend for a second time as an observer and engage in discussion about related matters.

Basic programme
The Basic Programme is divided into two parts. First, arrangements are made for the youth court panel member to visit a young offender institution and an attendance centre and also a variety of local authority, probation service and voluntary establishments for young offenders (see, generally, *Chapter 8*). Not earlier than six months after beginning to sit as a youth panel magistrate, the panel member should then continue this part of his or her training by participating in discussions dealing with

such subjects as curbing delay, remands, financial penalties, parental responsibility, community sentences and custodial penalties.

Refresher training

Refresher Training takes place during each three year term of the panel. It is designed to ensure that panel members remain aware of developments affecting their duties and in the field of youth justice generally.

New system

A Magistrates New Training Initiative (MNTI) will be phased in between 1 September 1998 and 1 September 1999 and will apply to magistrates newly appointed to youth panels at the annual election meeting in October 2000 and who will be commencing their panel sittings in January 2001. This new system is based on the competence principle, that is the need to demonstrate that someone can perform and continue to perform, a particular task to a required standard. Under the scheme, new members of the youth panel will still be required to complete relevant technical training courses. There will follow at a later date a system of appraisal to ensure that the new member of the panel has attained the necessary level of competence.

YOUTH COURT SITTINGS

When sitting to deal with cases, a youth court must consist of not more than three magistrates, and must normally include a man and a woman. If a stipendiary magistrate is present, he or she may sit alone, if it is considered inexpedient in the interests of justice to adjourn. If no man or woman is available, owing to unforeseen circumstances when the magistrates were chosen, or if for some reason the only man or woman present cannot properly sit as a member of the court, then—if an adjournment is not considered to be in the interests of justice—the case may proceed without a man or a woman (as the case may be).

In certain circumstances a single magistrate may act, e.g. when dealing with an application for an adjournment and remand (see, generally, *Chapter 7*).

CHAIRMANSHIP

Members of the youth court panel must elect, by secret ballot, a chairman of the youth court panel. They must also elect sufficient deputy chairmen to ensure that youth courts are capable of being properly constituted as described in the next paragraph. The relevant statutory rules are silent as to the term of office of the chairman and deputies, but the combined effect of the provisions suggests that it coincides with the three year life of the panel.

A youth court must sit under the chairmanship of the chairman or a deputy chairman. However, provided the elected chairman or a deputy chairman sits as a member of the court throughout the proceedings another member of the court can be allowed to take the chair—in effect 'under supervision'. If, for some reason which was unforeseen when the magistrates to sit were chosen, the chairman or a deputy chairman is not available, or he or she cannot properly sit as a member of the court (e.g. because of prior knowledge of the parties or relationship to a witness), the remaining members of the court must choose one of their number to preside.

LEGAL ADVICE

Youth panel magistrates are advised by a justices' clerk or other professional legal adviser and the position parallels that in the adult court. The independent nature of the justices' clerk's role[1] is emphasised by the Police and Magistrates' Courts Act 1994 under which the justices' clerk etc. is protected, in individual cases, from external direction in individual cases. The duties are also encapsulated in an earlier statute:

> It is hereby declared that the functions of a justices' clerk include the giving to the justices to whom he is clerk, or any of them, at the request of the justices or justice, advice about law, practice or procedure . . . including questions arising when the clerk is not personally attending on the justices or justice and the clerk may, at any time when he thinks he should do so, bring to the attention of the justices or justice any point of law, practice or procedure that is or may be involved in any question so arising.

This is reinforced by a *Practice Direction* issued by Lord Lane, when Lord Chief Justice, which makes it plain that the justices' clerk must ensure magistrates receive *all appropriate advice on law, sentencing, evidence, practice and procedure* and that relevant duties include advising:

- on questions of law or of mixed law and fact; and
- as to matters of practice and procedure.

The direction thus imposes a duty to advise *inter alia* on all guidance relevant to choice of penalty and decisions of the higher courts (including Court of Appeal guidance). A previous *Practice Direction* indicates that it may be appropriate to give information about disposals

---

[1] This independence is being further examined in an Access to Justice Bill

already imposed by the bench, or neighbouring benches, for similar offences. All legal advisers receive training in this regard.

The youth court retiring room
Where necessary, if magistrates adjourn to their private retiring room to consider a decision, it is good practice—when there are matters within the ambit of the *Practice Direction* and in all but the most straightforward cases—to consider seeking legal advice. Sometimes this will need to be at the outset—but the legal adviser must not accompany the magistrates as a matter of course (or if the decision is straightforward and does not involve legal or other relevant considerations). If the magistrates then require advice, the legal adviser should be audibly invited to join them with reasons being given. Nonetheless, the adviser is always entitled to go to the magistrates uninvited, and to give them such advice as appears necessary—but, if taking this course, should inform the parties what is going to be said. Where he or she has discussions with the magistrates after they have returned from retirement and they wish to retire again and on this occasion take the adviser with them, the parties should receive an explanation. The trend is towards giving advice in open court and in the full hearing of the parties. Otherwise, it is sound practice for the parties to receive an explanation and the chance to make appropriate further representations before the court comes to a final decision.[2]

SPECIAL PROTECTIONS AND PUBLICITY

For many years, youth courts were forbidden by law to sit in a room in which another type of court had been held within the hour, or was to be held within the hour. This legal restriction no longer applies but many magistrates' courts do have designated courtrooms for youth courts (where they are able to), sometimes with separate entrances and exits.

Who may be present in the youth court?
The principle of 'open court' does not apply to the youth court. Only the following people may be present:

- members and officers of the court
- parties to the case, their solicitors and counsel, witnesses and other people directly concerned, e.g. parents or guardians

---

[2] A detailed explanation of the justices' clerk's/legal adviser's role can be found in *The Sentence of the Court* (Waterside Press, 1998): see *Chapter 12* of that work, *Judicial Advice*.

- *bona fide* representatives of newspapers or news agencies (although there are restrictions on what they may write: p.50)
- such other people as the youth court may specifically authorise to be present on a given occasion.

Students who are pursuing youth justice-related courses or modules are frequently admitted to the youth court under this last head, as are researchers and other people with a *bona fide* interest. Trainee solicitors, probation officers and social workers accompanying their principal as part of their education would also fit into that category. It should be remembered, however, that there is no such thing as 'standing permission'. Authority to attend must be sought from the youth court on each occasion that it sits.

Naturally, the juvenile and his or her parents or guardian fall within the second category above, but in certain circumstances after a finding of guilt either can be required to withdraw: see p.67.

A move towards greater openness

The present government is committed to a wide-ranging programme for reform of the youth justice system and this includes as one of its objectives greater openness in youth court proceedings. It believes that youth courts should make full use of their wide discretion concerning who can attend proceedings. It is also encouraging the removal of the concept that victims often feel they are prevented from attending court to witness proceedings and therefore have no opportunity to understand decisions that are made or the consequences of these. The government considers it important that victims and the public have confidence in the outcome of proceedings. Factors which may argue against a victim, or victim's parents attending all or part of the court proceedings include:

- the age and vulnerability of the defendant
- the number of victims involved in the case; and
- the sensitivity or personal nature of information about the offender which may emerge, particularly at the sentencing stage.

None of these points would automatically lead to a decision not to admit attendance by a victim but they are considerations to be weighed in the balance as against the benefits of greater openness.

The government also believes that there is scope for the public to attend youth court proceedings, e.g. in cases where the nature of the offending has impacted on a number of people or a local community in general. Accordingly, it considers that there *are* circumstances in which it may be appropriate for members of the public to attend the youth court. Again, youth courts will need to consider each application carefully and individually, taking into account factors of the kind indicated above and weighing these against the benefits of openness. If a victim is refused permission to attend all or part of youth court proceedings, the court should, as a matter of good practice, explain the reason to him or her.

Restrictions on what the press may report

There are substantial and automatic restrictions on reports of proceedings of youth courts (section 49 CYPA 1933):

- no report can be published which reveals the name, address or school of any child or young person concerned in the proceedings
- neither can a report include any particulars likely to lead to the identification of any such child or young person
- no picture of a child or a young person concerned in the proceedings can be published or included in any programme.

The reference to being 'concerned in the proceedings' is a wide one, meaning that juvenile witnesses as well as juvenile defendants are protected from publicity.

Dispensing with the restrictions

The basic rule
The youth court can dispense with these requirements (with or without conditions) if satisfied that this is necessary to avoid injustice to the child or young person, or if such an individual is unlawfully at large and dispensing with the requirement may assist in their being returned to court.

This last dispensation only applies in limited circumstances, i.e. where a child or young person has been charged with, or convicted of, a violent offence, a sexual offence or an offence which, in the case of a person aged 21 years or over, is punishable with imprisonment for 14 years or more. The power cannot be exercised except upon application by, or on behalf of, the Director of Public Prosecutions (DPP: in practice through the Crown prosecutor) and unless notice of the application has been given to any legal representative of the child or young person.

The new 'public interest' criterion
Section 45 Crime (Sentences) Act 1997 amends section 49 of the 1933 Act above. The effect is to allow youth courts to dispense with the restriction on publication of reports of its proceedings where these relate to an offence of which the child or young person is convicted and where it is in the public interest to do so. The court should afford an opportunity for representations to be made before making an order to dispense with the restrictions. The new law *only* applies to offences committed on or after 1 October 1997.

In deciding whether to allow the identification of the juvenile, the court should have particular regard to the need to prevent further offending by him or her. Accordingly, lifting reporting restrictions could be particularly appropriate in cases where:

- the nature of the young person's offending is persistent or serious or has impacted on a number of people or his or her local community in general
- alerting other people to the young person's behaviour would help to prevent further offending by him or her.

On the other hand there will be circumstances in which the lifting of reporting restrictions will not be in the best interests of justice. Factors which courts will wish to consider are whether:

- naming the young offender would reveal the identity of a vulnerable victim and lead to unwelcome publicity for that victim
- publicity may put the offender or his or her family at risk of harassment or other forms of interference or harm
- the offender is particularly young or vulnerable
- the offender is contrite and has shown that he or she is ready to accept responsibility for their actions, e.g. by a timely/early guilty plea.

It should also be noted that a general discretionary power to impose press restrictions exists in all courts (e.g. the adult magistrates' court and the Crown Court) *whenever* a juvenile is involved in proceedings and in *whatever* capacity (section 39 Children and Young Persons Act 1933).

CHAPTER 5

The Youth Court: (2) Jurisdiction

The youth court is a magistrates' court specially constituted for the purpose of hearing charges against children or young persons. It also deals with certain other specified matters such as applications in respect of secure accommodation: see *Chapter 7, Remands and Bail*.

Since a youth court is a species of magistrates' court—itself a 'creature of statute' and only capable of doing what is prescribed by Act of Parliament or subsidiary legislation—the youth court cannot, on the face of things, deal with matters outside its basic remit unless jurisdiction has been legally assigned to it. The primary legislation in this regard is section 46 Children and Young Person Act 1933 (CYPA 1933). Thus, whilst a youth court may deal with criminal cases involving juvenile defendants, it remains debatable whether it can, e.g. deal with a complaint for a dog kept by a juvenile to be kept under proper control, or the new sex-offender and anti-harassment civil applications (*Chapter 8*) which must, seemingly, be dealt with in the adult court even though the respondent is a juvenile. Youth (and adult) court magistrates should take legal advice if faced with unusual items: ✋ 📖.

More generally, the youth court is bound by the same law as other magistrates' courts. Thus, all the standard rules of evidence and procedure apply unless specifically altered, enhanced or excluded by statute: see *Chapter 6, Procedures, Information and Evidence*.

CRIMINAL CASES

In relation to any criminal charge against a juvenile, except homicide, the youth court must usually deal with the matter, and whether defined as:

- a purely indictable offence (i.e. triable only in the Crown Court in the case of an adult: such as wounding with intent to do grievous bodily harm, rape, aggravated burglary); or
- an either-way offence (i.e. where, in the case of an adult, certain 'plea before venue'/'mode of trial' procedures would need to be followed in order to decide whether the case should be dealt with by the magistrates or the Crown Court: such as theft or assault occasioning actual bodily harm); or
- a purely summary offence (i.e. normally only triable by the magistrates' court: such as minor criminal damage, drunk and disorderly).

This basic rule that all cases must be dealt with in the youth court is subject to certain qualifications. These are dealt with on pp.53 to 60.

Changes in jurisdiction

As indicated in *Chapter 1*, the youth court and *not* the adult magistrates' court now deals with virtually all criminal allegations against people under 18 (prior to 1992 it was under 17). As a result of this and other jurisdictional changes it is essentially a *criminal* court dealing with people below the age of majority. If it were to transpire that sex offender and anti-social behaviour *civil* applications—or other civil matters—in respect of a juvenile *can* be dealt with in the youth court (perhaps as a result of a High Court ruling or legislation resulting from some European or Human Rights obligation), then the view that the youth court has an essentially criminal jurisdiction will need to be reassessed.

JUVENILES IN THE 'ADULT' COURT

As already explained, the general rule is that where someone below the age of 18 years appears or is brought before the court on any charge (other than homicide) he or she must be tried summarily by a youth court, and not by a magistrates' court or the Crown Court. There are a number of exceptions to this rule. Juveniles can be dealt with by a magistrates' court as follows:

- remands (e.g. a first remand when no youth court is sitting)
- where a juvenile is jointly charged with someone aged 18 or over
- when a juvenile is charged with aiding and abetting an adult, or other secondary participation in a crime alleged against someone aged 18 or over (or vice-versa)
- where the offence arises out of circumstances which are the same as, or connected with, those giving rise to an offence with which someone aged 18 or over is charged.

It should be noted that whenever a juvenile appears in a magistrates' court that court has power under section 39 CYPA 1933 to direct that information revealing his or her identity must not be published.

Remands

An adult court may deal with a remand application in respect of a juvenile, especially where no youth court is sitting at the relevant time and place: see, generally, *Chapter 7, Remands and Bail*. This applies whether or not the juvenile is jointly charged with an adult. For remand purposes, people aged 17 and over are subject to adult powers so that they can, e.g. be held in a remand centre or prison.

Juveniles jointly charged with adults

Where a juvenile and an adult are charged jointly with an offence, then the venue for dealing with the case must be the adult court in the first instance. It is not essential that the word 'jointly' or 'together' are used in the actual charge. Thus, e.g. if a 20 year old unlawfully enters premises to commit a burglary and uses a 15 year old as the 'look-out' both defendants could be charged with burglary before the adult court.

Juvenile aiding and abetting an adult, etc.

The adult court *may* hear a charge against a juvenile who is charged with aiding or abetting, counselling or procuring, allowing or permitting an offence alleged against someone aged 18 years or over—or where an adult is charged with aiding or abetting etc. an offence by a juvenile.

Juvenile and adult connected by an offence

The adult court *may* hear a charge against a juvenile where it arises out of circumstances connected with an offence with which an adult is charged. Thus, e.g. if an adult is accused of theft and the juvenile is accused of handling the property allegedly stolen, the charge against the juvenile can, at the court's discretion, be heard by an adult magistrates' court.

Remittal by the adult court to the youth court after a finding of guilt

One tenet of the provision of specialist youth courts is that they are better equipped to deal with juveniles taking into account the special considerations and factors affecting this age group outlined in *Chapter 8*. By virtue of section 56 CYPA 1933, if a juvenile is being dealt with in the magistrates' court (e.g. charged jointly with burglary with an adult: see above), then if the juvenile pleads guilty or is found guilty, the case *must* be remitted to the youth court acting for the place, or covering the area, where he or she habitually resides. There is an exception to this rule where the adult court is satisfied that such a remittal would be undesirable and that the case can be dealt with by one of the following methods:

- a discharge (absolute or conditional)
- a fine (subject to the normal youth court maxima: see *Chapter 8*)
- binding over the parent or guardian.

The adult court can make these disposals as well as appropriate ancillary orders: compensation, costs, driving licence endorsement, etc.

Remittal to the youth court where the juvenile pleads not guilty

Where, in any of the connected matters described above the adult pleads guilty but the juvenile pleads not guilty, the adult court may remit the juvenile for trial in the youth court. A similar result may follow where the adult court is deciding whether there is sufficient evidence to send an adult to the Crown Court for trial—and either does so (or discharges the adult) but continues to deal with the juvenile who enters a plea of not guilty. In such circumstances, the juvenile is left 'high and dry' on his or her own to be tried in the magistrates' court—and, again, there is a discretion to remit the case to the youth court for trial.

Committal to the Crown Court where connected with an adult
Even where an offence is defined as triable either way (i.e. when an adult can be tried by the magistrates' court or by the Crown Court depending on the outcome of mode of trial procedures) a juvenile has no right to elect to be tried by jury at the Crown Court. Accordingly, the normal rule is that a juvenile charged with an indictable only offence (other than homicide) or an either way offence should be dealt with in the youth court. However, there are circumstances in which the court would want to commit the case to the Crown Court for trial. This would include where the juvenile is charged jointly with an adult and the court considers it necessary in the interests of justice to proceed with a view to committing both defendants to the Crown Court. A practical illustration of this might be where both defendants are denying the offence and the adult offender exercises his or her right trial by jury at the Crown Court. The adult court (or the youth court if the juvenile appears before it at a different time) could decide that a single venue for the trial (i.e. the Crown Court) is the most appropriate option: 📖🖐.

In such circumstances, the juvenile could also be committed to the Crown Court in respect of any other indictable offence which is linked with the joint matter. An example might be the alleged commission by the juvenile of a wounding offence whilst trying to escape apprehension during a joint burglary: 📖🖐.

The High Court has ruled that the word 'jointly' should receive a liberal interpretation and could cover such situations as where one offender in an aggravated vehicle-taking offence was the driver and the other the passenger. It has also indicated there is no requirement that the juvenile and adult need appear in court together at the time the mode of trial decision is made: 📖🖐.

THE CROWN COURT AND 'GRAVE CRIMES'

The Crown Court has power to sentence a juvenile to long term detention in certain limited circumstances. This power exists by virtue of section 53 CYPA 1933, which enables the Crown Court to order a longer period of detention than its normal maximum (two years in a young offender institution: *Chapter 8*). An order under section 53 imposed by the Crown Court means that the juvenile is detained in such a place and in such conditions as the Secretary of State directs (subject to early release on licence). This can be a local authority establishment (e.g. a secure unit), a youth treatment centre or a Prison Service establishment.

Long term detention may only be ordered by the Crown Court if it is of the opinion that none of the other methods by which the case could be dealt with are suitable. In the main, grave crimes are homicides (where the youth court cannot in any event deal with the case) and offences punishable in the case of an adult with 14 years imprisonment or more (when it has a discretion whether to deal with the case or not). Examples of such '14 year' offences include:

- arson (criminal damage by fire)
- burglary of a dwelling (burglary of other premises is excluded since the maximum sentence in the case of an adult is ten years imprisonment)
- aggravated burglary
- rape and attempted rape
- robbery
- wounding with intent to do grievous bodily harm.

The law was amended in 1991 so as to include indecent assault on a woman and, yet more recently, an allegation against a young person (not a child) that he or she has caused death by dangerous driving, or by careless driving whilst under the influence of drink and drugs. None of these additions are '14 year' offences.

'Grave crimes': the youth court's decision

Since, in most cases, there will be no adult offender connection, the juvenile will appear first in the youth court. A decision is made there before the case starts as to whether the matters should be committed to the Crown Court so that that court can consider the long-term detention provisions of section 53 if the juvenile is found guilty. This is often referred to as 'mode of trial', but the section 53 procedure must be distinguished from mode of trial in the adult court in relation to either way offences (which does not apply to the youth court or to juveniles).

Under section 53, the youth court must, in effect, make a sentencing prediction—balancing the desirability of keeping a juvenile under 18 years of age out of long-term custody if found guilty against the public interest in ensuring that serious offences are properly punished.

In a leading case of *R v Fairhurst* (1986) certain guidelines were laid down to assist youth panel magistrates in making this sentencing prediction and to assist judges in sentencing. It should be emphasised that this ruling occurred at a time when the maximum young offender institution period in the Crown Court for relevant juveniles was 12 months (and not two years as it is now).

Fresh guidance

Fresh guidance on the inter-relationship between long-term detention (Section 53) and detention in a young offender institution (present maximum term of two years: *Chapter 8*) was given by the Court of Appeal in *R v AM* and related appeals in 1997. The differences between the two types of custodial sentence were emphasised in that detention direct to a young offender institution by the court can be imposed on offenders aged 15, 16 and 17 but not on those aged 14 for any imprisonable offence. On the other hand detention in respect of grave crimes is available for those aged 14 to 17 and younger, but only on conviction of specified offences as indicated above. Apart from the two year maximum for detention in a young offender institution, it is also subject to a two month minimum period—whereas under section 53 there is no maximum or minimum.

This 1997 ruling also confirmed that the Crown Court might send someone direct to a young offender institution where an offender of 15, 16 or 17 had been convicted by magistrates of an offence punishable on indictment for a term exceeding six months and the magistrates had committed him for sentence. On the other hand, detention on the basis of a grave crime could only be ordered where the offender had been convicted in the Crown Court on indictment.

Furthermore, the Court of Appeal endorsed a statement in *R v. Fairhurst* that a balance was to be struck between the objectives of keeping young offenders out of long-term custody on the one hand and, on the other, the need to impose sufficiently substantial sentences on people who committed serious crimes so as to provide both appropriate punishment and a deterrent to protect the public. However, the Court of Appeal disagreed with the *Fairhurst* ruling in so far as it had been stated that if the offence would merit a sentence of less than two years but more than 12 months for an offender of 17 or over, then the sentence should normally be one of youth custody and not detention under section 53. The Court of Appeal further stated that the Crown Court should not exceed the two year limit without much careful thought; but if it concluded that a longer—even if a not much longer—sentence was called for, then it should impose whatever it considered the appropriate period of detention as a grave crime.

It is thus most important that justices on the youth panel, when considering a mode of trial hearing for a youth, should pay particular regard to whether the Crown Court may need to exercise its special powers to detain under Section 53 of the CYPA 1933: generally ✋ 📖.[1]

Accommodation of young people ordered to be detained under s. 53

The arrangements for accommodating young people held under section 53 are made by HM Prison Service on behalf of the Home Office. However, the Prison Service consults with the Department of Health about the placement of offenders aged 16 or under, and they are usually placed in secure facilities which form part of the child care system.

Young people made subject to section 53 orders usually spend most of their sentence in secure conditions. Placements can be in prison service young offender institutions for those aged 15 or over, the youth treatment centre at Glenthorne or in local authority secure accommodation. The introduction of secure training orders has added to the options available to the youth panel (*Chapter 8*). However, many conditions have to be met before a secure training order can be made, and cases will still arise where a youth has committed a grave crime but does not fulfil the conditions for a secure training order. In these instances consideration will still have to be given to the use of section 53 of the 1933 Act ('grave crimes'): ✋ 📖.

Correct sequence of events

In *R v Herefordshire Youth Court, ex parte J* (1998), *The Times*, May 4 it was emphasised that decisions on venue must be made *before* pleas are taken. There was an onus on the court legal adviser and the prosecutor to consider the gravity of the offence and to draw the question of mode of trial to the attention of the bench before any pleas are taken.

Homicide

Any offence involving a juvenile charged with homicide *must* be sent to the Crown Court for trial. The term 'homicide' means 'unlawful killing'—including such offences as murder and manslaughter. There is legal opinion that it also includes causing death by dangerous driving.

Grave crimes and additional offences

Where a case involving a grave crime is committed to the Crown Court the youth court, since the Crime and Disorder Act 1998, need not delay passing sentence in relation to other less serious matters whilst the Cro̶ t deals with the grave crime. Previously, such lesser matters ̶urned pursuant to a ruling of the higher courts.

̶ whether section 53 can ultimately survive a 1999 ruling of the ̶o the effect that children should not be tried in an adult court.

Changing the mode of trial decision

The youth court has power in certain circumstances to change a decision to deal with a case itself (i.e. to alter its mode of trial decision). These are all unusual situations: ✋📖. Conversely, if a court has decided to proceed summarily, the decision can be changed at any time prior to the end of the prosecution evidence. Normally there will be some fresh circumstance. Where the court has decided to commit the case to the Crown Court (i.e. grave crime) it may review this decision at any time up to the date of the actual committal of the case to the Crown Court.

ON BECOMING AN ADULT

Sometimes juveniles aged 17 will have their next birthday during the youth court proceedings. If, e.g. the offence is indictable only (i.e. triable only at the Crown Court in the case of an adult, such as robbery) the question for the youth court is whether or not it retains jurisdiction.

The basic rule

The basic rule is that if the youth court has already agreed to hear the matter and there are no fresh circumstances, then it must retain jurisdiction.

Adult either way matters

Where the alleged offence is one which is triable either way in the case of an adult (e.g. theft, assault occasioning actual bodily harm) the answer will depend on whether mode of trial has been determined and recorded. Thus, e.g. if a 17-year-old enters a not guilty plea and the court adjourns to a pre-trial review or a trial date, then the attainment of 18 years of age will not affect the court's power to proceed with the case itself. Neither can the defendant, on attaining 18, suggest that he or she is entitled to claim trial by jury. It would be otherwise if the court had not embarked on the case: ✋📖.

New powers concerning remittal for trial or sentence

The Crime and Disorder Act 1998 contains a provision which states that where someone who appears or is brought before a youth court charged with an offence *subsequently attains the age of 18*, the youth court may, at any time:

(a) before the start of the trial; or
(b) after conviction and before sentence

remit that person for trial or, as the case may be, for sentence to a magistrates' court acting for the same petty sessional area as the youth court.

This new provision would prevent the difficulty that a youth court experienced in *R v. Uxbridge Youth Court, ex parte Howard*, Queens Bench Division, March 1998 (*Justice of the Peace Reports*, 327). In this case, a defendant aged 17 was due to appear before a youth court for the first time, having been charged with a summary offence. He failed to attend. A warrant was issued for his arrest and he attended after he had become 18. The case was adjourned and subsequently remitted to the adult court. It was held that there was no power for a youth court to remit a case to an adult magistrates' court.

REMITTING AS BETWEEN YOUTH COURTS

If a juvenile has been found guilty by a youth court in a different area to that where he or she habitually resides, that court may remit the case to the youth court for the area where the juvenile habitually resides. The remitting court may grant bail or remand the juvenile in custody.

The juvenile has a right of appeal against any order of the home court (i.e. the receiving court) as if he or she had been found guilty by that court. Where the juvenile originally pleads guilty and subsequent to remittal applies to change that plea, the receiving court may accept the change of plea and go on to hear the case: *R v Stratford Youth Court, ex parte Conde, The Times*, 5 April 1996.

It should also be noted that normally adult courts and Crown Courts are, after a finding of guilt, obliged to remit to the juvenile's local youth court unless satisfied that this would be undesirable. For the adult court's own sentencing powers in respect of someone convicted there as a juvenile (e.g. because they were jointly charged with an adult) see p.54.

CHAPTER 6

Procedures, Information and Evidence

This chapter looks at a number of key procedural and evidential rules, including certain special rules which apply only in relation to the youth court. It also examines the factual basis for decisions-making through solid information. An underlying theme is that, at all points in the youth justice process, sound decision-making depends upon having relevant, up-to-date, good quality information to work with. Among other things, this chapter explains what information the youth court needs before considering an order in respect of a juvenile. Analogous information will be relevant at earlier stages.

Procedures affected by age
Chart 2 in *Part III* of this handbook gives details of *Some Procedures Affected by Age* (with chapter references where appropriate).

BRINGING A JUVENILE TO COURT

Proceedings are started in the youth court in the same way as in the adult court, i.e.—following on from the investigation process outlined in *Chapter 2* under the heading *Police*—by:

- the police (or other prosecutor) laying an *information* followed by the issue of a *summons* or—more rarely—a warrant of arrest in the first instance; or
- the juvenile being charged by the police. Where the juvenile is *charged* he or she may be bailed to appear before the court at a specified time and place. Alternatively, he or she may be brought to court direct from police custody, having been held in local authority accommodation if police detention prior to charge was for a lengthy period: see, generally, *Chapter 7, Remands and Bail.*

Where the police proceed by laying an information, an application is made to the justices' clerk's office asking for a summons to be issued requiring the juvenile and his or her parents or guardians to attend a sitting of the youth court at a time and on a date set out in the summons. Prior to laying an information or charging a juvenile, the prosecutor must notify the appropriate local authority and also a probation officer for the area in which the court sits (in effect, in future, the local Youth Justice Team: YOT). This triggers the various procedures and responsibilities which were outlined in *Chapter 2*.

The juvenile must normally be present at court

Only in a limited number of situations will a case be dealt with in the absence of a juvenile. If the juvenile does not attend on the hearing date, consideration will be given to issuing a warrant for failure to appear, subject to proof of service of the summons or, as the case may be, the court being satisfied that the defendant was bailed to attend on the date in question. There is an exception to the practice of requiring the juvenile's attendance where the written plea of guilty procedure in relation to lesser matters has been invoked by the prosecutor: see later in this chapter under the heading *Written Guilty Pleas*.

REDUCING DELAY

In 1996, it reportedly took

- an average of 142 days between arrest and sentence for persistent young offenders; and
- an average of 131 days from the date of the offence to completion of the case in respect of all young offenders.

The government has indicated its determination to end these delays which it says

> . . . impede justice, frustrate victims and bring the law into disrepute. Delays do no favours to young offenders themselves: they increase the risk of offending on bail and they postpone intervention to address offending behaviour. The top priority will be to halve the time taken between arrest and sentence for persistent young offenders by fast-tracking them through the system.

A number of areas have now begun operating fast track schemes for persistent young offenders and most of these have proved successful in reducing some of the delays. The government believes that other provisions in the Crime and Disorder Act 1998 will, when operational, implement the pledge to halve the time taken to sentence persistent young offenders and ensure permanent improvements across England and Wales. These will enable cases in which a straightforward guilty plea is anticipated to be heard within a few days of the juvenile being charged. They will promote the effective management of the pre-trial preparation of cases, since certain powers will be exercised by a single justice rather than by the full bench. It is also expected that these powers will be delegated where appropriate to justices' clerks. The government considers that statutory time limits together with the adoption of best practice will create conditions in which delays should be reduced significantly. It anticipates that time limits will cover most of the period from arrest to sentence. Whether the government achieves its stated objective remains to be seen. Many practitioners feel that unless there are effective sanctions against the prosecutor or the defence for failing to meet time limits or deadlines, then complete success is unlikely to materialise.

ATTENDANCE OF PARENT, GUARDIAN ETC

The white paper *Crime, Justice and Protecting the Public* which preceded the Criminal Justice Act 1991 stated that

> . . . attendance at court is a powerful reminder to the parents of their duty both to their children and to the wider community. It marks the degree of responsibility which the law regards parents as having for the behaviour of their children in this age group. A court appearance is a major event in the life of a young person. Parents who take their responsibilities seriously would wish to make every effort to attend, whether or not the law requires them to do so. Some do not. The Government believes that parents should always attend court with their children, unless there is some overriding reason why they cannot. (para. 8.7)

It is essential for the parent to attend where the juvenile is *under the age of 16* unless the court considers that it would be unreasonable to require attendance in all the circumstances. Some youth courts insist on both parents attending in view of considerations of the size or type of financial orders and the arrangements for payment of these. Other factors may include the desirability of a parental bind over: see *Chapter 8*.

If the parent or guardian does not attend the court may need to consider adjourning, with a written warning to do so on the new date, or even issuing a warrant. Whether the juvenile or parent fails to attend, magistrates should always seek advice if considering a warrant: 📖✋.

A local authority with parental responsibility and actually looking after a relevant juvenile should send a representative of its social services department to the hearing. This, it can be suggested, will not necessarily be covered by the attendance of a social services member of the YOT since the provision envisages someone with responsibility for the child's day-to-day care. An exception exists where the juvenile is actually living with his or her parent or guardian (which occurs when the juvenile has been allowed to live at home by the local authority).

MEASURES TO ASSIST THE JUVENILE

The welfare principle, mentioned in *Chapters 1* and *8*, is the guiding standard for decision-making in youth courts, a fact emphasised by certain requirements in the Magistrates' Courts (Children and Young Persons) Rules 1992 which, among other things, require the court to assist the juvenile in putting forward his or her case and to understand the proceedings. In the procedural rules, the juvenile is referred to either as a 'minor' or the 'relevant minor'.

Legal representation
In many cases, defendants in the youth court will be legally represented (often by way of legal aid: below). This should ensure that explanations are made to the juvenile inside and outside the courtroom and that any defence or mitigation is properly discerned and presented to the court.

Role of the parent or guardian
The parent or guardian must be allowed to assist the juvenile in conducting his or her defence where the juvenile is not legally represented (this e.g. will include the cross-examination of witnesses for the prosecution).

Explanations
It is standard practice in many youth courts for there to be an explanation to the juvenile and his or her parents at the start of the proceedings about who is present, what the role of each person is and how the hearing will be conducted. In keeping with this approach, it is also common for the physical locations of practitioners and other people in the courtroom to be marked in some way, e.g. 'Magistrates', 'Court clerk', 'Prosecutor', 'Defence Solicitor'.

The court has a duty to explain the substance of the charge in simple language and subject to the age and understanding of the juvenile. The duty is usually, in practice, discharged by the legal advisers, but this is a matter for local decision. This broad duty is in addition to any specific requirements to make explanations by virtue of individual Acts of Parliament in relation to particular aspects of procedure, e.g. there are various requirement to explain aspects of custodial sentences, community sentences and bail decisions.

As explained in *Chapter 5*, the youth court has exclusive jurisdiction over most criminal cases involving juveniles (unless the case falls within the exceptions described in that chapter). The youth court will take a plea by asking whether the juvenile pleads 'guilty' or 'not guilty'. As in all court proceedings, the court must be satisfied that the defendant understands the nature of the allegation which is being made (although there is no longer, as there once was in the case of a juvenile under the age of 14, any need to consider the *doli incapax* rule: see p.21). Similarly, in accordance with the general law, a youth court must ensure that any plea of guilty is correctly entered and that it is not equivocal—when the court should refuse to accept it (e.g. where the defendant pleads guilty to handling stolen goods and then states that he or she had no idea the property was stolen). Similarly, if the juvenile admits the offence but on a factual basis which the prosecutor cannot accept, there will need to be a 'Newton hearing' (a trial and determination of that particular issue): 📖✥. The age of the defendant is one reason for paying careful attention to all these aspects.

NOT GUILTY PLEA

In the case of a juvenile who indicates a plea of 'not guilty', the court must hear the evidence of witnesses in support of the charge. The rules of evidence and order of proceedings are essentially the same as in the adult court. Certain special rules affecting the giving of evidence by juveniles are mentioned at pp.78-79. There are several deviations from the standard adult rules of procedure, primarily designed to involve the juvenile and his or her parents in the hearing, to ensure that he or she understands what is happening and to secure a sound information base for decision-making. Where the juvenile is not legally represented or assisted by his or her parents, and instead of asking questions by way of cross-examining he or she makes assertions (such as 'He kicked me first'), the court must put to the witnesses such questions as it thinks necessary on the juvenile's behalf. For this purpose, the court may question the juvenile in order to bring out or clear up any points arising out of the assertions that he or she is making.

PRIMA FACIE CASE AND DEFENCE

If it appears to the court that a *prima facie* case is made out, the child or young person—if he or she is not legally represented—must be told that they may give evidence or address the court, and the evidence of any defence witnesses must then be heard. This is by virtue of rule 9 of the 1992 Rules. The juvenile must also be told that there is a right to remain silent but that the court may draw such inferences as appear proper from failure to give evidence: see p.79 and 📖✥.

Whether or not the juvenile gives evidence, he or she is entitled to call defence witnesses and if not legally represented the court may assist by putting questions to these witnesses. The defendant will normally give evidence *before* any other defence witnesses.

Once all the evidence has been heard, the youth court magistrates must decide whether the prosecution case is proved beyond reasonable doubt, i.e. to the same high standard which applies in the adult court.

For unsworn evidence and the 'promise' aspect of *The oath*, see under that heading in the *Evidence* section later in this chapter.

PROCEDURE AFTER A FINDING OF GUILT

Following a finding of guilt, the procedure laid down in the Magistrates' Courts (Children and Young Person) Rules 1992 is the same whether the juvenile *pleaded guilty* or he or she was *found guilty* by the court after hearing the evidence. Once this stage is reached the youth court must dispose of the case by making one or more of the orders described in *Chapter 8, Sentence and Orders of the Youth Court*. Before doing so a variety of matters must be considered.

Making a statement
The juvenile and his parent or guardian, if present, must be given the opportunity to make a statement. This could apply even if the relevant minor is legally represented: but the advocate's views should be sought.

Previous findings of guilt
As a matter of practice, any previous findings of guilt and related orders are cited to the court by the prosecutor, including any warnings or reprimands given by the police (see under next heading). It is for the court to decide what effect, if any, previous findings of guilt have upon the seriousness of the present offence or the need to protect the public from serious harm from the offender: see, generally, *A note on previous convictions and responses etc*, pp.95-96.

Reprimands and warnings
Reprimands and warnings are discussed in *Chapter 3* where the details which will in future be given at the sentencing stage are noted (see p.43). The prosecutor, in presenting reprimands, warnings and old style cautions to the court, should ensure that they are in a format which distinguishes between these items and occasions when the juvenile has been found guilty of an offence by a court. The best practice is for the two types of record to be presented in separate lists, preferably on separate sheets. As indicated in *Chapters 3* and *8* a conditional discharge is normally barred by statute where the present offence was committed within two years of an earlier police warning.

Pre-Crime and Disorder Act 1998 old-style cautions may also be submitted on a separate sheet/list, but not purely informal warnings.

General conduct
The court must take into consideration such information as to the general conduct, home surroundings, school record and medical history of the

juvenile as may be necessary to enable it to deal with the case in his or her best interests, including preventing future offending. In particular the statutory rules refer to the duty of the local education department, social services department or probation service to supply information. There is a general obligation on local authorities to provide information to the court about juveniles who are charged with criminal offences (*Chapter 2*). In practice, most information is provided not under this wide-ranging rule but by means of pre-sentence reports (PSRs) prepared by social workers or probation officers: see under the heading *Pre-sentence Reports*, below. If, for any reason the information is not available, the court will need to consider an adjournment for reports to be prepared. In future, the arrangements will be via the local YOT.

Withdrawal of relevant minor or parent or guardian

Rule 10 of the 1992 Rules enables the youth court, if it considers it necessary in the interests of the juvenile, to require him or her or his or her parents or guardians to withdraw from the court during part of the proceedings. This may be to discuss sensitive information with the parent in the absence of the juvenile or vice versa (it may be because the relevant minor might be more forthcoming in discussing certain issues in the absence of the parent).

It is impossible to be prescriptive about the types of sensitive information which will justify reliance on this rule. These will vary from such items as the defendant or a parent suffering from a terminal illness to aspects of the parents' lifestyle that are questionable or which are not known to the relevant minor.

Duty to explain manner in which the court proposes to deal with the case and the effect of any order

An illustration of the need for particular care when dealing with juveniles is contained in rule 11 of the 1992 Rules. This rule is designed to ensure that the juvenile and any parent or guardian has the opportunity to comment on what is being proposed. Rule 11 provides:

(i) before finally disposing of the case or before remitting the case to another court in pursuance of section 56 of the Act of 1933, the court shall inform the relevant minor and his parent or guardian, if present, or any person assisting him in his case, of the manner in which it proposes to deal with the case and allow any of those persons so informed to make representations; but the relevant minor shall not be informed as aforesaid if the court considers it undesirable so to do.

(ii) on making any order, the court should explain to the relevant minor the general nature and effect of the order unless, in the case of any order requiring his parent or guardian to enter into a recognisance, it appears to it undesirable so to do.

This general duty to explain the court's intentions is in addition to any specific duty under statute to give reasons or explanations for youth court decisions: see *Reasons for Decisions* later in this chapter and the individual sentences and orders outlined in *Chapter 8.*

PRE-SENTENCE REPORTS (PSRs)

Under the original version of the Criminal Justice Act 1991, the requirement to obtain PSRs—prepared for the case under consideration—before making most types of community order or imposing a custodial sentence, was, for all practical purposes, obligatory in the youth court. Changes introduced under the Criminal Justice and Public Order Act 1994 gave courts a discretion to dispense with a PSR if they considered it unnecessary for such a report to be provided. However, there is an important rider to this in the case of a juvenile offender whereby a court may only dispense with a PSR if it has considered an existing one on the offender concerned (i.e. in effect one prepared for a different, earlier hearing). If more than one earlier report exists then the most recent one must be considered.

In view of the fact that the situation and circumstances of a juvenile can change quite rapidly, it will normally be prudent to have a fresh and completely up-to-date PSR prepared whenever the court is considering a custodial sentence or a community sentence in respect of that juvenile.

PSRs are prepared by a representative of the local authority social services department (i.e. a social worker) or a probation officer: the arrangements being made via YOTs when formally in place: *Chapter 2.*

Written reports
PSRs must be in writing—although this does not preclude extra oral information if circumstances so dictate, e.g. fresh developments in the juvenile's circumstances. In addition, some areas now provide oral assessments to the youth court of a young person's suitability for some community orders where the level of intervention activity is small. Rule 10 of the 1992 Rules confirms that any written report of a probation officer, local authority, local education authority, education establishment or registered practitioner may be received and considered by the court without being read aloud. The PSR contents will have been explained to the juvenile out of court by (or on behalf of) the report writer. This may mean reading it out in private to someone who cannot read or using an interpreter if the offender's first language is not English. A copy is given to the offender and his or her lawyer. The court must ensure that the offender understands the effect of all information received by it—as explained earlier in this chapter.

Availability of reports
Rule 10 further provides that the court must arrange for copies of any written report to be made available to:

(a) the juvenile's legal representative, if any;
(b) any parent or guardian who is present at the hearing, and;
(c) the juvenile (except where the court may otherwise direct on the grounds that it appears impracticable to disclose the report having regard to his or her age and/or understanding or it is undesirable to do so having regard to serious harm which might thereby be suffered by the juvenile).

Where the juvenile is not legally represented and a report has not been made available to him or her or read aloud, he or she must always be told the substance of any part of the information given to the court which has a bearing on his or her character or conduct *and* which the court considers to be material to the manner in which the case should be dealt with *unless* it appears impractical to do so, having regard to his or her age and understanding. This applies whether or not the minor is asked to withdraw during any part of the proceedings.

In comparable circumstances a parent or guardian, if present, must be told the substance of any part of such information which the court considers material and which makes reference to his or her character or conduct or to the character, conduct, home surroundings or health of the juvenile.

If, having been given this information, the person affected by it wishes to respond (e.g. to challenge its accuracy or any implications which flow from the information) by producing evidence of their own, the court—if it thinks that this extra evidence would be material—must adjourn the proceedings for it to be produced. It must also, in the case of a report which would be affected, require the attendance at the adjourned hearing of the report-maker.

Nature and relevance of a PSR
The PSR is a central decision-making tool in relation to all serious offences. By statutory definition, a PSR is a report in writing which:

(a) with a view to assisting the court in determining the most suitable method of dealing with an offender, is made or submitted by a probation officer or by a social worker of a local authority social services department; and
(b) contains information as to such matters, presented in such manner, as may be prescribed by rules made by the Secretary of State.

The preparation and content of PSRs are subject to a Home Office *National Standard for Pre-Sentence Reports* (that government department having responsibility for probation service provision). A special section of the standard deals with 'Reports on Young Offenders' as follows:

34. While all the PSR standard applies to youth court report writers there are particular considerations which must be borne in mind which are set out below.

35. Where a PSR is being prepared on a *child or young person* the report writer must take into account section 44 of the Children's and Young Persons Act 1933 which requires the court to have regard for the welfare of the individual. The United Nations Convention on the Rights of the Child to which the United Kingdom is a signatory also requires that in all actions concerning children, i.e. those below 18 years, in courts of law the best interests of the child shall be the primary consideration. The report writer should therefore take account of the age of the young offender and his or her educational circumstances.

36. In considering possible proposals, the report writer should have particular regard to the individual's maturity where it has an influence on offending or the risk of reoffending. In the case of 16 and 17 year olds the report writer should consider which of the sentences available to the youth court is most suitable to the individual offender.

37. Where the young offender is of school age, in every case the report writer should obtain information from the school, pupil referral unit or local education authority, concerning a pupil's attendance, behaviour and performance, for use in the *relevant information about the offender* section of the report. In cases where the court orders additional information from the school, this should be attached to the PSR.

38. A PSR written on a child or a young person should also take account of any *care plan* prepared for that individual under the Children Act 1989 and must address the child or young person's relationship with his or her parent(s) or person(s) with parental responsibility and the degree to which they are responsible for the child or young person and should be involved in any supervision. Where a PSR is being prepared on a child or young person it will usually be desirable for the parent to be interviewed as well as the offender. Under the Criminal Justice Act 1991 the parents or guardian of a young offender aged under 16 will be required to attend court with their child unless the court considers it unreasonable to do so. Where the offender is 16 or 17, his or her parents or guardian may be required to attend.

39. Under the 1991 Act . . . courts are under a duty to bind over the parents of a young offender under 16 to take proper care of him or her and exercise proper control . . . where they think it is desirable in the interests of preventing offending. The courts have a power to bind over the parents of offenders aged 16 or 17. Where the young offender is subject to a Community Order, courts can further bind over parents to ensure that the children comply with the order's requirements. PSRs have an important role to play in providing information and advice to

the courts which can help them to decide upon the desirability or otherwise of proposing a bind over. The factors which may be relevant to such a decision include:

- whether the juvenile is likely to benefit from increased supervision and intervention by parents
- whether the parents' authority and control over the juvenile would be strengthened
- whether the parents are physically in a position to exercise the necessary degree of care and control (e.g. the juvenile may be living away from the parents) and
- the circumstances of the present offence.

40. The PSR writer should bear in mind that under the 1991 Act the court has a duty to order the parents of guardian to pay any financial penalties imposed on their children aged under 16 unless it considers it unreasonable to do so. The court has the power rather than a duty to order the parents to pay the penalty in the case of 16 and 17 year old offenders.

The *National Standards* have been adopted by report writers from social services departments (a comparable standard, but issued jointly, applies to supervision orders).

In cases where a PSR is obtained, it forms part of the relevant information which the court should consider *before* finally deciding on such important matters as the seriousness of the offence or offences, restriction of liberty and suitability for a particular community order. Amongst other things, PSRs contain information about what demands will be made on the offender by a given community order. PSRs are also relevant in relation to the risk of the offender re-offending—both generally, but more particularly in relation to the protection of the public from serious harm from the offender where the court is dealing with a sexual or violent offence (see *Chapter 8*).

Once a PSR is ordered and an adjournment allowed for it to be prepared, the report writer will—under *National Standards*—aim to produce a report which is impartial, balanced and factually accurate. PSRs in the youth court are nowadays usually prepared within a maximum of 15 working days.

The report writer will bear in mind that the report is for the court alone, and that it does not represent the interests of any individual or organization. He or she will provide a professional assessment of the case, the nature and the cause of the offence or offences and a note of any action which can be taken to reduce re-offending.

The *National Standard* confirms that a PSR must always be provided if requested by a court; this despite the fact that an offender might refuse to assist in its preparation. In such an event, the writer will aim to produce the most useful report possible, ensuring that the offender was offered at least two opportunities for an appointment. The writer will, in any event, take all reasonable steps to obtain available, relevant information about the offender and his or her circumstances.

The PSR writer will normally check whether the juvenile is due to appear in the youth court on other matters, so that sentencing can take place at the same time where reasonably practical.

To accord with the *National Standard,* a PSR must be clear, concise, free of jargon, coherent and accurate in grammar, syntax and spelling. The report will start by setting out basic information on the front sheet, following which information will appear under the following main headings:

- an introduction
- offence analysis
- relevant information about the offender
- an assessment of the risk to the public of re-offending
- a conclusion.

Critically, for the youth court, the offence analysis will normally include:

- an analysis of the offence or offences, including an assessment of the offender's culpability and a degree of pre-meditation
- information about aggravating or mitigating features of the offence, which might assist the court when assessing seriousness (the PSR will not actually use the terminology of aggravation or mitigation)
- an assessment of the context of the offence including information about any relevant associated offences
- a note of the offender's motivation with the aim of helping the court to understand why the offender committed the offence or offences
- an assessment of the consequences of the offence, i.e. the actual damage, injury, harm, cost of the offending (including the impact on the victim)
- an assessment of the offender's attitude to the victim, the offence, awareness of its consequences and any expressed remorse or guilt, and any desire to make reparation and/or provide compensation
- an assessment of any special circumstances, e.g. family crisis, alcohol, drugs, physical or mental health directly relevant to the offending. The report will draw attention to ways in which these might be relevant to 'seriousness'
- where there is a specific feature of the offence which seems to conform to a pattern of previous offending (e.g. targeting of vulnerable victims), this should be included.

As part of the *offence* analysis the report writer will form a view about how serious the offence is—so as to ensure that the restriction of liberty contained in any proposed community sentence is commensurate with the offence. The writer will be steered by any provisional indications of seriousness given by the court.

Information about the *offender* is critically relevant to assessing the suitability of particular community orders for the offender: the PSR summarises the offender's personal and social circumstances, and evaluates any pattern of offending identified in the light of these. This part of the PSR covers offending history and deals with issues of relevance to section 29 Criminal Justice Act 1991 with regard to previous findings of guilt or failures to respond to earlier orders: see *Chapter 8.*

Whilst the relevant provisions post-date *National Standards,* there will be a need, in future, to deal with any attempts at rehabilitation pursued via the youth offending team (YOT) and linked to a police warning: *Chapter 3.*

Overall, the PSR should give a balanced picture of the offender, good or bad, noting any positive action taken by him or her since the offence.

Where a community sentence is envisaged
It is the practice of the youth courts to avoid giving indications of the likely final disposal of a case before considering the contents of the PSR. However, to assist report writers, provisional indications of seriousness may be given subject to a clear rider that the court wishes to keep all its options open. Seek information/advice about the local practice: 📖.

Where the PSR envisages a probation or supervision order, or combination order—see *Chapter 8*—it should contain an outline of the proposed supervision plan. Whenever community orders are proposed, there should be a description of the purposes and desired outcomes, the methods to be used, the timetable with targets for achieving objectives, the intensity of supervision envisaged, and the likely effect on other members of the juvenile's family. The description of any proposed programme should indicate the degree of restriction of liberty involved, how the disposal will help tackle the behaviour which led to the offence, and the steps to be taken if the offender does not comply. If a community order requires consent (not now a general requirement: *Chapter 8*), the report should deal with willingness to comply.

Unless the court has specifically asked for the report to cover a number of options, any proposal will be for a single order—with an explanation if other options have been considered and rejected.

Confidentiality
PSRs are confidential documents, and the information in them is limited to what is relevant to the court's decision. When a custodial order is

made, a copy is however normally provided for the probation service/social services department in the custodial institution to assist in the order being carried out and with release arrangements.

SCHOOL REPORTS

As already indicated in the extract from *National Standards* above, the PSR will deal with information from the juvenile's school where he or she is of school age. It is an express requirement following a finding of guilt (whether by plea of guilty or after a trial) for the court to take into account all available information about general conduct, home surroundings, school record (where the offender is still at school) and medical history. Historically, in the case of the school, this was usually a separate school report and all too often quality and liaison arrangements were variable. [1] Whilst practice differs, such information will now more often than not appear only in the body of the PSR and be collated by the PSR writer (unless, perhaps, there is some unusual reason for submitting a free-standing school report). It is relevant that someone nominated by the chief education officer will be part of the local YOT.

MEDICAL REPORTS

Before deciding whether to make certain types of order the court must receive and consider appropriate medical and psychiatric reports: see *Chapter 8* under the heading *Mental Disorder*. This is a specialist area and mental disorder is itself a highly complex subject, not least when it comes into contact with the criminal law. Magistrates should seek legal advice, particularly if such issues arise in the youth court: 📖✍.

OTHER REPORTS

The Crime and Disorder Act 1998 will, when fully operational, bring in a number of new measures. Some of these such as reparation or action

---

[1] Research by NACRO (*School Reorts to the Juvenile Court: Could Do Better,* 1986) indicated that such reports could contain information about behaviour in school, including educational problems and truancy, which might have no direct relevance to offending, but which could 'attract the attention' of the court. Authors of PSRs therefore need to check what information is received from the school — as should lawyers acting for juveniles. It is important that such information relates to valid sentencing considerations. A DfEE consultation paper currently canvasses returning to separate school reports.

plan orders require courts to obtain information, but it may not be necessary to require that information in the context of a full scale PSR.

Chapter 8 covers parenting orders. These are to help and support parents to control the behaviour of their children. They will require parents to attend counselling and guidance sessions and could require them to make sure their children go to school each day. Before the court makes a parenting order, it must obtain information about the parents' family circumstances and the likely affect of the order on these. What form this information should take, i.e. whether it should be oral or written information will be a matter for the court to decide, depending on the circumstances of the case. There is no statutory requirement for a written report and a court might chose to rely on an oral report made in court. The different circumstances which may trigger a parenting order will determine which agency has to obtain the necessary information.

Reparation orders are new measures to be piloted as a result of the 1998 Act. They make young offenders face up to their crimes and the consequences of their actions. They could involve, e.g. writing a letter of apology to a victim, apologising in person, cleaning graffiti or repairing criminal damage. Again, the details appear in *Chapter 8.* However, before a court can make a reparation order, it must obtain and consider a written report. The report writer may be a member of the local YOT, a social worker in the local authority's Social Services Department or a probation officer. The choice of report writer may depend on the nature of the individual case or the local arrangements for providing court reports.

Crime and Disorder Act 1998 measures to be piloted also include action plan orders—short, intensive programmes of community-based intervention, combining punishment, rehabilitation and reparation. They last three months and are designed to address the specific causes of offending. Before a court can make an action plan order it must obtain and consider a written report. Again, the report writer may be a member of the local YOT, a social worker in the local authority's Social Services Department, or a probation officer. The choice of report writer may depend on the nature of the individual case or the local arrangements for providing court reports.

Generally speaking, YOTs (*Chapter 2*) are responsible for co-ordinating arrangements for the provision of reports to the courts. The YOT should, therefore, take the lead locally in identifying a report writer so as to ensure timely delivery of all types of report to the court.

REASONS FOR DECISIONS

Courts are required to give reasons for certain decisions, such as the decision that only custody can be justified, and to explain any such decision to the juvenile in ordinary language. Where it is obligatory to give reasons, youth courts must also cause the reason to be entered in the court register and to be specified in any relevant warrant of commitment. The main circumstances in which reasons must be given are:

- when imposing a custodial sentence (*Chapter 8*)
- when the youth court does not award compensation in cases where it has such a power (*Chapter 8*)
- in relation to the remand of a juvenile to prison or local authority accommodation with a requirement of security. Most remand decisions such as remands on conditional bail and remands in custody neccessitate giving reasons to support the court's decision (see *Chapter 7*)
- when a youth court declines to bind over a parent or guardian of an offender under the age of 16. It must then state in open court that it is not satisfied, having regard to the circumstances of the case, that the exercise of the bind-over power would be desirable in the interests of preventing the commission by the juvenile of further offences and why it is not so satisfied
- when a youth court makes a reduction in sentence because of a guilty plea (*Chapter 8*) it must state in open court that it has done so.

There are other circumstances where, although reasons do not have to be given as a matter of law, the court is bound to explain the decision, its meaning and e.g. the effect of a breach of the order—when it will need to do this in ordinary language. These situations include when an order of conditional discharge is made, or a probation order or curfew order (when this last disposal is fully in force): see, generally, *Chapter 8*.

Some courts adopt a practice of giving reasons and explanations when making any order, subject to the age and understanding of the juvenile. The need to explain in ordinary language connotes a need to explain in language that the juvenile can understand. Skill in making such an explanation lies in understanding the communication needs of juveniles of different ages and levels of maturity.

LEGAL AID

In view of the nature of the special care that is required in dealing with juveniles, many young people accused of either-way or indictable offences are granted legal aid under the 'interests of justice' criterion (below) to enable them to be represented by a lawyer. The complex legal provisions which pervade youth court powers and procedures and the need for a high degree of sensitivity to the welfare principle and preventing offending point to the need to take a broad view here.

Either the juvenile or his or her parent may make an application for the requisite legal aid order. In the first instance, the application will usually be considered by the justices' clerk or a person duly authorised by him or her. They will require a statement as to the juvenile's and the parent's means if the juvenile is under 16 years of age. An application can also be made orally in court, but this will usually be referred to the justices' clerk for appropriate details to be taken and calculations made.

The legal aid order will cover representation in respect of the youth court proceedings and advice in respect of a possible appeal.

The same legal aid regulations that cover the adult court apply to legal aid in the youth court subject to certain refinements. Hence, there must normally be a completed application form and evidence of means such as wage slips from the parent, or if in receipt of state benefits evidence such as a stamped letter of confirmation from the Benefits Agency.

A legal aid order may be made provided the person considering the application is satisfied that both: (a) disposable income and disposable capital are such that the juvenile is eligible for legal aid;[2] and (b) it is in the interests of justice that a legal aid order should be made.

Any doubt as to whether the juvenile ought to receive legal aid should be resolved in the juvenile's favour.

If legal aid is granted it may be subject to a contribution order from the juvenile, but more frequently from the parent. This is usually out of disposable income, payable weekly.

On the rare occasions that legal aid is refused in respect of a juvenile, the matter can, where an either-way or indictable only offence is alleged, be reconsidered by the Area Legal Aid Committee in certain circumstances. An alternative 'appeal' against refusal in respect of legal aid for an either-way or indictable offence could be to the court or a justice of the peace. This would preclude further review by the Area Legal Aid Committee unless within a 14 day time limit.

In respect of the refusal of legal aid for a purely summary offence (e.g. drunk and disorderly) then following refusal by the justices' clerk the only avenue of review is to a justice of the peace or the court.

When the youth court is considering imposing a custodial sentence there is an obligation to grant legal aid if applied for subject to exceptional circumstances: 📖✍.

---

[2] The Access to Justice Bill could do away with means testing for all courts and with any form of contribution order other than in the Crown Court (where there could be a possible contribution *at the end of the proceedings*)

WRITTEN GUILTY PLEAS

Section 12 Magistrates' Courts Act 1980 concerning written pleas of guilty by post in relation to summary offences carrying a maximum penalty in the case of an adult of not more than three months imprisonment (often called 'MCA cases' or 'paper pleas') has been extended to 16 and 17 year olds in the youth court.

This procedure relates only to 'summons cases' and is at the discretion and instigation of the prosecutor. If the prosecutor decides to adopt the procedure, the juvenile is served with a 'statement of facts' relating to the offence and may submit a written plea of guilty—with details of financial circumstances and mitigating circumstances—in the same manner as in the adult court. The matter may then be dealt with in his or her absence. If the plea is equivocal or the court requires the presence of the offender, the matter will be adjourned.

In practice the procedure has been rarely invoked in the youth court. Whilst of value in relation to road traffic offences, those involving juveniles often resulted in a warning or a caution and hence no court proceedings. However, under the new system of warnings and reprimands this may have to change, as dealing with such matters repeatedly will no longer be legally permissible: see *Chapter 3*.

The need to consider the welfare principle can also be an inhibiting factor in that, under general principles affecting the youth court, there is a need for that court to consider welfare factors. Similarly, the juvenile and his or her parents or guardians should be involved in proceedings when the juvenile is being prosecuted, even for less serious offences such as minor acts of disorder. It seems, however, that in extending the written plea procedure to 16-year-olds (it already applied to 17-year-olds), Parliament could hardly have intended that either prosecutors or courts should hesitate to use a method which avoids the possible escalation of a minor matter into some deep rooted inquiry into the juvenile's background and general behaviour.

EVIDENCE

Various special rules apply to the giving of evidence by juveniles. These are of general application, not specifically referable to the youth court and are not dealt with here. Typically, they concern the situation where a juvenile gives evidence in the adult court or Crown Court against an adult alleged to have committed offences against the juvenile. On the whole, the provisions are designed to protect the juvenile from the trauma of facing the alleged perpetrator or being subjected to what can be insensitive/aggressive cross-examination. There are provisions concerning video-recorded evidence, television links and 'notices of transfer' under which cases can be sent to the Crown Court for trial without juveniles having to give evidence at the magistrates' court stage.

The promise
Children under 14 years of age do not take the oath or affirm. They give unsworn evidence. The oath taken in the youth court by any witness of 14 and over differs from that used by adults in magistrates' courts:

> I *promise* before Almighty God to tell the truth, the whole truth and nothing but the truth.

Seemingly, this is to prevent the use of the word 'swear' by juveniles. The rules regarding alternative forms of oath according to religious belief and those concerning the right to affirm instead of taking the oath are the same as in the adult court. Anyone who wishes—and asks—to affirm instead of promising to tell the truth may do so.

Abolition of the rebuttable presumption that a child is doli incapax
As already noted, section 34 Crime and Disorder Act 1998 abolished the rebuttable presumption of *doli incapax* for 10 to 14 year olds: see p.21.

Effect of a child's silence at trial
A court can, as a result of section 35 Crime and Disorder Act 1998, draw any appropriate inferences from the failure of a juvenile to give evidence or answer questions at his or her trial. This now applies to all people of ten or over: generally 📖✍.

A NOTE ON APPEALS

A juvenile found guilty and/or sentenced by a youth court (or magistrates' court) can appeal to the Crown Court against the finding and/or sentence. Alternatively, they may appeal to the High Court by way of case stated (i.e. on a point of law) or apply to that court for a judicial review of the youth court's decision.

Appeal to the Crown Court is the normal avenue, especially in sentencing matters. The offender must give written notice within 21 days of being sentenced, setting out the general grounds of appeal, e.g. 'That in all the circumstances the sentence was too severe'. Similarly, rights are conferred on parents and guardians where they have had orders made against them. The Crown Court rehears the case in full and can confirm the youth court's decision or substitute its own sentence. This may be a less severe sentence or a heavier one—but limited to the youth court's maximum powers of punishment.

CHAPTER 7

Police and Court Remands and Bail

The terms 'adjournment' and 'remand' are often confused and used incorrectly. The proceedings (or cases) are *adjourned*; the defendant is *remanded*. When a case is adjourned the court normally has a *discretion* whether to simply adjourn or, when doing so, to remand the defendant as well. It will usually remand the defendant where he or she is charged with more serious matters, especially if previously bailed to appear at court by the police, or where he or she has been brought to court by the police in custody. A remand may be on bail or in custody. This standard terminology applies equally to adults, children and young persons.

Generally speaking, when someone is remanded there is a right to bail unless certain criteria set out in the Bail Act 1976 apply; but there are also restrictions on the grant of bail. The court makes the ultimate decision, regardless of whether there is a measure of agreement between the prosecutor and the defence. It must give reasons for refusing bail or when conditions are attached to a grant of bail. All these matters are outlined later in this chapter.

Many juvenile arrest cases begin in the adult court if no youth court is sitting/available when the juvenile is first brought to court. Subsequent hearings then normally take place in the youth court, provided the case does not involve an adult also: see *Juveniles jointly charged with adults, Chapter 5*. Whether in the adult court or youth court, adjournments and remands can be dealt with by a single magistrate.

RELEVANCE OF AGE

The bail provisions in relation to juveniles do not depend on the normal youth court age range, but on whether or not the defendant has reached the age of *17 years*. From age 17 upwards the adult provisions apply (as they also do to 17 year olds in police detention under the Police and Criminal Evidence Act 1994 (PACE): see *Chapter 2*). Thus, when decisions about police detention or police or court bail are made in the case of a juvenile who is already 17, he or she will be dealt with, for these purposes, as if an adult. The choice will lie between bail with or without conditions, and a remand into custody (a prison or a remand centre). The local authority accommodation or secure accommodation provisions described later in this chapter are only available for people below 17 years of age.

In the case of a juvenile under the age of 17, any remand will be on bail (with or without conditions), into local authority accommodation or, in certain very limited circumstances into custody. This residual power to remand some juveniles to custody is being phased out.

The court must inquire about the age of the juvenile and, if necessary, hear appropriate evidence. The age of the juvenile is as presumed or declared by the court: see *Chapter 1* under *Establishing age and related matters*. No order or judgement of the court is invalidated by later proof that the age is not as so stated.

BAIL

The Bail Act 1976 (as amended) applies to the remand of juveniles and both the 1976 Act and PACE governs the way in which the police consider issues surrounding the detention of juveniles and their release or otherwise from that detention, with or without bail.

Bail by a police officer

Section 38 of PACE provides that where someone aged ten to 16 years is charged with an offence (otherwise than under a warrant endorsed for bail), the police custody officer shall order his or her release from police detention, with or without bail, unless:

(a) his or her name or address cannot be ascertained or the custody officer has reasonable grounds for doubting whether a name or address furnished by him or her as his or her name or address is his or her real name or address;

(b) the custody officer has reasonable grounds for believing that the person arrested will fail to appear in court to answer to bail;

(c) in the case of a person arrested for an imprisonable offence, the custody officer has reasonable grounds for believing that the detention of the person arrested is necessary to prevent him or her from committing an offence;

(d) in the case of a person arrested for an offence which is not an imprisonable offence, the custody officer has reasonable grounds for believing that the detention of the person arrested is necessary to prevent him or her from causing physical injury to any other person or from causing loss of or damage to property;

(e) the custody officer has reasonable grounds for believing that the detention of the person arrested is necessary to prevent him or her from interfering with the administration of justice or with the investigation of offences or of a particular offence,

(f)   the custody officer has reasonable grounds for believing that the detention of the person arrested is necessary for his or her own protection; or

(g)   the custody officer has reasonable grounds for believing that he or she ought to be detained in his or her own interests.

Where a custody officer authorises an arrested juvenile to be kept in police detention, the officer must secure that he or she is moved to local authority accommodation, unless the officer certifies:

(a)   that, by reason of such circumstances as are specified in the certificate, it is impracticable to do so; or

(b)   in the case of an arrested juvenile who has attained the age of 12 years that no secure accommodation is available and that keeping him or her in other local authority accommodation would not be adequate to protect the public from serious harm from him or her.

Definitions

'Local authority accommodation' means accommodation provided by or on behalf of a local authority (within the meaning of the Children Act 1989). 'Secure accommodation' means accommodation provided for the purpose of restricting liberty; and any reference, in relation to an arrested juvenile charged with a violent or sexual offence, to protecting the public from serious harm must be construed as a reference to protecting members of the public from death or serious personal injury, whether physical or psychological, occasioned by further such offences committed by that person. Where an arrested juvenile is moved to local authority accommodation, it is lawful for any person acting on behalf of the authority to detain him.

Where bail is granted by the police

Where bail is granted by the custody officer this can be *unconditional* or *conditional*. The power to grant police bail is longstanding. Since 1995 the custody officer's powers have been widened to enable him or her to grant bail, broadly speaking, upon the same kind of conditions that magistrates can impose. Such conditions can only be imposed where deemed necessary to prevent the juvenile from absconding, committing an offence, or interfering with witnesses or otherwise obstructing the course of justice. However, the police do not have power to require someone to reside at a bail hostel, to make themselves available for inquiries or reports or to undergo medical tests. The police have a power to require someone to give security before being released on bail in any circumstances.

Since the introduction of this provision, the appearance of juveniles from police detention simply so that bail conditions can be imposed by the magistrates has been significantly reduced—and with it the need for 'special courts' outside normal hours.

When the custody officer grants conditional bail, the juvenile may ask the same or another custody officer to vary the conditions. The officer must keep a record of any bail conditions and give reasons for imposing them. A juvenile may also apply to the court for conditions to be varied before the first hearing, or at any later stage.

Where a juvenile charged with an indictable offence (the relevant definition includes both purely indictable offences such as murder and also either way offences such as theft and assault occasioning actual bodily harm) has been given bail with conditions, these may be re-considered and the court has power to rescind or vary the conditions, impose conditions of bail (if conditions were not imposed previously) or indeed withhold bail.

General right to bail at court
The general right to bail in section 4(1) Bail Act 1976 applies subject to certain exceptions. These include:

- where the juvenile has been arrested for breach of bail conditions or for absconding, or because a surety (see the explanation below) has withdrawn
- where the court is satisfied that the juvenile should be kept in custody for his or her own welfare
- if he or she is in custody by virtue of a sentence of a court.

As in the adult court, bail may also be refused provided that a statutory ground for this exists and the court announces a reason in support of that ground. The most common grounds are that there are substantial grounds for believing that:

- the defendant will fail to surrender to custody
- the defendant will commit an offence if released on bail
- the defendant will interfere with witnesses.

The grounds and reasons must also be recorded in the court register and the defendant must be given a copy of them. It should be emphasised that these basic Bail Act procedures apply in addition to any special provisions in relation to juveniles as described elsewhere in this chapter.

Unconditional bail
If a juvenile is remanded on straightforward unconditional bail by a court, the only obligation is to surrender to the custody of the court on a

given day and at a fixed time (sometimes called 'answering to bail'). Failure to do so may result in a warrant of arrest being issued and proceedings for the separate criminal offence of failing to answer bail under section 6 Bail Act 1976.

Conditions of bail imposed by a court

Before or after release on bail, the juvenile can be required to comply with conditions of bail. The purpose of bail conditions is to ensure that the juvenile surrenders to custody, does not offend whilst on bail, does not interfere with witnesses or otherwise obstruct the course of justice and, where appropriate, makes himself or herself available for the purpose of inquiries or a report.

If a court imposes conditions, varies conditions or refuses bail, it must give its reasons. These must be written into the court register and a copy must be given to the defendant.

Sureties and security

Before being released on bail, a juvenile may be required to provide a *surety*, i.e. someone prepared to vouch that the juvenile will attend court at the end of the remand period by entering into a recognizance and thereby risking forfeiture of a sum of money fixed by the court if the juvenile later fails to surrender to bail. Similarly, someone may be required to give *security* (i.e. deposit money or something else of value) for the juvenile's surrender to the custody of the court on pain of losing the money or other item of value.

Where a parent or guardian stands surety for a juvenile, that person may be required to ensure that the juvenile complies with any requirement to which the parent or guardian has consented. This cannot apply where the juvenile will reach age 17 before he or she is required to surrender to custody. The maximum sum for this purpose is £50.

Where a recognisance is entered into for the appearance of a juvenile at court, and the juvenile fails to appear as required, then the court must immediately declare the automatic forfeiture of the recognisance and issue a summons to the surety to appear before the court to explain why that person should not pay the sum involved. The court then has a discretion as to whether all, part or none of the sum involved should be paid. If the surety fails to answer the summons, the court may proceed in his or her absence, provided that the summons has been served.

Special rules for certain offences

If a juvenile is charged with actual or attempted murder, manslaughter, rape or attempted rape, and has a previous finding of guilt for any of these offences, or for culpable homicide (an offence in Scotland), he or she may be granted bail only if the court—or indeed a constable as applicable—is satisfied that there are exceptional circumstances to justify taking this course. If the previous finding of guilt was for manslaughter or culpable homicide, this provision will only apply when the juvenile was ordered to serve either detention in a young offender institution or long-term detention under the CYPA 1933: see, generally, *Chapter 5* under *Grave Crimes* and *Chapter 8, Sentences and Orders of the Youth Court*.

Arrest for breach of bail

A juvenile who has been bailed, with or without conditions, may be arrested by a police constable if that constable reasonably believes the accused is not likely to answer, i.e. surrender, to bail. In addition, if bail has been granted with conditions, the constable may arrest a person who the constable reasonably believes is likely to break any of the conditions, or if he or she suspects that a condition has been broken. If a surety has been accepted (above) and notifies the constable that the person is unlikely to answer to his or her bail and the surety wishes to be relieved of their duty, the constable may also arrest the juvenile.

Where a juvenile is arrested for this reason, the court must form a view about whether he or she is likely to surrender to custody or has broken or is likely to break a bail condition. This is meant to be a straightforward procedure. It may be dealt with by a single magistrate, not necessarily a member of the youth court panel, and not necessarily in the youth court. As in all bail proceedings, the normal rules of evidence do not apply, but fairness dictates that both parties (the prosecutor and defendant) are given an opportunity to state their case. There is no need for evidence on oath, even where the juvenile denies the breach—albeit evidence is sometimes given, or required by the court in practice.

There is no power to adjourn such a case. The court must decide whether it is of the opinion that the arrested juvenile is not likely to answer bail or has broken, or is likely to break, a condition of bail. If the court feels unable to form such an opinion, then it must order that the defendant be released on bail on the same conditions as originally imposed. The police have power to arrest a juvenile who fails to report to a police station to answer police bail.

LOCAL AUTHORITY ACCOMMODATION

If bail is refused to a juvenile up to and including the age of 16 years, he or she must generally be remanded to local authority accommodation. This is accommodation provided by or on behalf of the local authority (e.g. a county council or metropolitan authority) in accordance with the Children Act 1989.[1]

The court must designate the relevant local authority. If the juvenile is already being looked after by a local authority, that particular authority must be designated. In other cases it will be the local authority for the area where the court believes the juvenile to reside, or where the offence was allegedly committed. Where a court has remanded a 15 year old or 16 year old male into local authority accommodation it may, on the subsequent application of that authority, declare him to be remanded into custody if certain provisions apply: see *Remands in Custody* below.

Remands into local authority accommodation with requirements

Instead of a simple remand into local authority accommodation, the court, when remanding a juvenile in this way can, *after consultation with the local authority:*

(a) impose a requirement on the local authority, stipulating that the juvenile must not be placed with a named person;
(b) require the juvenile to comply with any such conditions as could be imposed when granting conditional bail (except conditions as to residence);
(c) impose on the local authority requirements with a view to securing compliance with conditions.

Provision is now also made for a juvenile in breach of such provisions to be arrested by a police constable and brought before the court for the position to be further considered. Any decisions of the court to impose conditions on the juvenile must be explained in ordinary language, and written into the court register and in the warrant of commitment.

SECURE ACCOMMODATION[2]

Secure accommodation means accommodation which is provided in a community home, a voluntary home or a registered children's home for the purposes of restricting liberty. Secure accommodation cannot be used by a local authority for more than 72 hours without an order of the court.

---

[1] The local authority does not thereby gain *parental responsibility* in relation to the juvenile: which would have significant implications for the authority and the parents or guardians of the child going far beyond the purposes of the remand.

[2] Changes to this outline of *Secure Accommodation* are brought about by sections 97 and 98 Crime and Disorder Act 1998 (when in force). Readers are referred to the extended explanation at page 166 of this work: 📖✍.

The proceedings are governed by section 25 Children Act 1989, and the Secure Accommodation Regulations 1991. An application can be made by a local authority in respect of a juvenile under 17 years of age who is detained under PACE or remanded in local authority accommodation, provided that the juvenile:

(a) has a history of absconding, is likely to abscond from non-secure accommodation and, if he or she absconds, is likely to suffer significant harm, or

(b) if kept in any other accommodation is likely to injure himself or herself or other people.

However, different criteria apply where the remanded juvenile:

(a) is charged with or has been convicted of
    (i) a violent or sexual offence, or
    (ii) an offence punishable with 14 years imprisonment or more, or

(b) has a recent history of absconding while remanded to local authority accommodation, and is charged with or has been convicted of an imprisonable offence, alleged or found to have been committed whilst so remanded.

In this event, the local authority must establish that any accommodation other than secure accommodation is inappropriate because:

(i) the child is likely to abscond from such other accommodation, or
(ii) the child is likely to injure himself or other people if kept in any such other accommodation.

The local authority looking after the child must give notice of the application to the court, indicating the grounds for the application, the names and addresses of persons to whom they have also given notice of their intention to make an application, and the date, time and place of the hearing. Jurisdiction is conferred on the court which has remanded or committed the juvenile to local authority accommodation. The juvenile must have been informed of his or her rights to apply for legal aid.

At the hearing of this application the court must explain the nature of the proceedings and, if the juvenile is unrepresented, assist the juvenile in the conduct of the proceedings. The local authority may address the court and then call evidence. The juvenile's case is then heard and, following a closing speech, the court must determine whether or not the criteria are satisfied. Where it is so satisfied, a report may be considered. If the application is adjourned an interim order can be made. In announcing the order the court must explain it to the juvenile in ordinary language. In the case of a juvenile who has been remanded, the maximum period of the authorisation is the period of the remand, but where the juvenile is committed to the Crown Court for trial (see *Chapter 5*) the order for renewal may be for a maximum of 28 days.

REMANDS IN CUSTODY

Where a 15 or 16 year old male is refused bail, he will normally be remanded into local authority accommodation (above)[3] but may in certain circumstances be remanded into custody and to a prison. When section 23 CYPA 1969, as amended by the Criminal Justice Act 1991, is implemented, such remands will be abolished, in theory, when local authorities have made sufficient provision of secure accommodation. Before a remand into custody can take place, a number of conditions have to be satisfied:

(a) the alleged offender must be *male* and have attained the age of 15 years
(b) the court must have consulted with either a probation officer or a social worker of a local authority
(c) the juvenile must be legally represented, or have applied for legal aid which was refused on the grounds that his means were sufficient. (Unless he has failed to apply for legal aid)
(d) the juvenile must have been charged with, or found guilty of, a sexual or violent offence, or an offence punishable with 14 years imprisonment in the case of an adult, or he must have had a recent history of absconding while remanded to local authority accommodation, and be charged with or found guilty of an imprisonable offence, alleged or found to have been committed, while he was so remanded
(e) the court must be of the opinion that only remanding him to a remand centre or prison would be adequate to protect the public from serious harm from him.

The Court must explain to the offender, in ordinary language, why it is of that opinion, openly in court. The reasons must be recorded in the court register, and in the warrant of commitment.

The term 'serious harm' is explained in section 23(13) CYPA 1969 in relation to sexual and violent offences as referring to the protection of members of the public from death or serious personal injury, whether physical or psychological, occasioned by further such offences committed by the juvenile.

---

3 See Footnote 1

Again, it should be remembered that for remand purposes a 17 year old juvenile is dealt with as if he or she were an adult (see above).

OTHER REMAND CONSIDERATIONS

Remand into the custody of a constable ('police custody')
Where a court has power to remand a juvenile in custody, then such remand may be to the custody of a constable for a period of up to 24 hours. In effect, this means a remand into police custody. Such a remand may only be for the purpose of inquiring into other offences (i.e. not any with which he or she has already been charged). If such a remand is ordered, the juvenile must be returned to court as soon as the need to inquire into other offences has ceased.

A 17 year old can be so remanded for up to 72 hours. If the need for the remand ceases, then again the alleged offender must be returned to court sooner.

Committal for sentence
If a defendant aged 17 or over (whether male or female) is committed to the Crown Court for sentence because the youth court is of the opinion that the juvenile should be sentenced to a greater period of detention than it has power to impose (see *Chapter 8* under *Committal for Sentence*), section 37 Magistrates' Courts Act 1980 provides that a remand otherwise than on bail will be to a remand centre or prison. Where the defendant is under 17, a remand otherwise than on bail will be into custody.

Abolition of committal to Crown Court for sentence The power to commit to the Crown Court for sentence will be repealed when Schedule 10 Crime and Disorder Act 1998 is brought into force. To date, the schedule is not in force: 📖✍.

Bail information schemes
Bail information schemes are operated by the Probation Service and often in relation to juveniles by, or in conjunction with, a local authority social services department (in future YOTs could perform this function). In practice, the bail scheme worker will speak to the juvenile in custody prior to the first court appearance and obtain as much relevant information about him or her as possible. Liaison will then take place with interested parties, including the defendant's solicitor, his parents and the Crown Prosecution Service. Information provided as a result of this is designed to assist all concerned to provide the court with the fullest possible details so that an appropriate remand decision to be made at the next hearing.

Prosecution right of appeal in bail decisions
Under the Bail (Amendment) Act 1993, the Crown prosecutor has a right to appeal against certain decisions of the court to grant bail where a remand has been sought otherwise than on bail. For the provisions to apply the juvenile must be charged with or found guilty of an offence punishable in the case of an adult with imprisonment for five years or more, or an offence of taking a conveyance or aggravated taking of a motor vehicle. Appeal is to a Crown Court judge. Pending appeal the juvenile will remain in custody or local authority accommodation as appropriate despite the magistrates' decision to release him or her.

Remands into custody for up to 28 days before plea
The provisions of sections 128 and 128A Magistrates' Courts Act 1980, allowing further remands into custody to take place in the absence of the defendant with consent, or remands into custody for more than eight days on a second appearance, presently apply only to people aged 17 years or above. The Criminal Procedure and Investigations Act 1996 applies these provisions to people below the age of 17: .

Further remands of children and young persons
Where a youth court has remanded a juvenile for information to be obtained in respect of him or her, any youth court acting for the same petty sessional division or place may, in his or her absence, extend the period for which he or she is remanded, but if this occurs the juvenile must appear before a court or a magistrate at least once every 21 days. When the information is obtained, the youth court may deal with the juvenile finally.

Reconsideration of decision to grant bail
If, since bail was granted, new information has come to light or there has been a change of circumstances in the case of a juvenile charged with an indictable or either-way offence, the Crown prosecutor may apply to the court for bail to be withdrawn or for bail conditions or additional conditions to be attached. This applies to both court bail and police bail. Notice of the application must be given to the defendant.

Offences committed whilst on bail
Quite apart from the fact that if offences are committed whilst on bail this adversely affects the likelihood of bail in the future, it should be noted that an offence committed when on bail must, by law, be treated as more serious by virtue of that fact: *Chapter 8.*

For an extended explanation of the changes noted in *Footnote 2* on p.86, see p. 166.

PART TWO

CHAPTER 8

Sentences and Orders of the Youth Court

CONTENTS

Section

CHAPTER 8

Sentences and Orders of the Youth Court

In broad terms, sentencing in the youth court parallels that in the magistrates' court[1]—subject to certain special rules. There is a wider range of orders; and there are restrictions or limitations on the use of some of these. The precise age of the offender within the ten to 17 age band is often critical when considering what powers are available: see also the *Explanatory Charts* in *Part III* of this handbook.

I: GENERAL CONSIDERATIONS

The underlying principles of sentencing—including those which flow from the sentencing framework introduced by the Criminal Justice Act 1991 (as amended)—are the same as for adults. In summary, sentences:

- must be commensurate with the seriousness of the current offence (or that offence and other offences associated with it). This principle is sometimes described by saying that the sentence must be proportionate to the offence.
- for a sexual or violent offence (see pp.136-137), in so far as custody is concerned, can also be passed on the basis that only such a sentence would be adequate to protect the public from serious harm from the offender.

Most penalties in the youth court are imposed on the basis of the seriousness of the offence—the 'just deserts' approach introduced by the Criminal Justice Act 1991. There are three key stages. The court must:

- form a view about the general level of seriousness of the offence
- then look at the facts of the actual *offence* considering any aggravating factors (i.e. those which make it more serious than others of its type) or mitigating factors (which make it less so)
- finally, apply this in the context of the individual *offender*. This involves taking account of factors directly referable to the offender, including any personal mitigation. But the court should also bear in mind that it is dealing with a juvenile:
  - to whom welfare considerations apply: see under the heading *Welfare, Just Deserts and Preventing Crime* in *Section II* of this chapter

---

[1] For a general overview, see *The Sentence of the Court* (Waterside Press, 1998)

- who is young and possibly immature (juveniles can be 'younger' or 'older' than their years, physically, emotionally or intellectually)
- who may be socially, educationally or otherwise disadvantaged; and
- who is at a critical stage in his or her personal development and vulnerable to a variety of influences.

At the first stage above there are *Four Levels of Sentence*: see *Section IV* of this chapter. So far as the second stage is concerned, factors which make an individual offence more or less serious are often included in penalty guides produced locally (and have been promulgated nationwide, e.g. via the *Magistrates' Association Sentencing Guidelines* and *National Mode of Trial Guidelines*, both designed for adults). There are, at present, no specific national guidelines for the youth court and thus adult guidelines have to be applied by analogy and with appropriate allowances/adjustments for youth court factors as described in this handbook. The welfare principle and the fact that juveniles mature at different rates in particular—as well as the fact that many juvenile offenders have scant financial or other resources—make the formulation of such guidelines difficult. Nonetheless, the Magistrates' Association is currently considering whether to devise guidelines for the youth court.

An offence committed whilst on bail must, by law, be treated as more serious by virtue of that fact (see, generally, *Chapter 7*) and similarly a racially aggravated offence.

As to the final stage, certain examples of *offender* based factors are contained in *Section V* of this chapter under *Community Sentences*.

At appropriate points in this decision-making process, the youth court will want to bear in mind the principal statutory aim of preventing offences by children and young persons as declared by section 37 Crime and Disorder Act 1998.

General principles of sentencing

As already indicated, the same principles which underpin sentencing in magistrates' courts and the Crown Court also apply in the youth court—subject to the special and additional considerations described in this handbook. Historically, there have been six traditionally recognised objects of sentencing which courts must try to achieve. These are:

- punishment
- reparation (including financial compensation to a victim)
- protection of the public
- deterrence
- reflecting proper public concern
- rehabilitation.

These principles must nowadays be pursued in the light of the 'just deserts' approach to sentencing introduced by the Criminal Justice Act 1991, and in the case of the youth court the welfare principle and the principal purpose of youth justice, preventing offences: *Section V.*

Making reparation, i.e. putting something back by way of acts intended to benefit the victim or the community is an underlying rationale of community sentences, particularly community service: see *Section V* of this chapter. The fact e.g. that an offender has made voluntary reparation may indicate remorse or contrition and thereby, depending on the circumstances, justify some reduction of sentence. Compensation to victims of crime is one aspect of reparation and is a constant sentencing consideration: see *Section VI.*

In one of the first cases to come before the Court of Appeal following the 1991 Act, the late Lord Taylor, Lord Chief Justice, sought to clarify whether deterrent sentences were consistent with proportionality in sentencing, i.e. whether they had been superseded by that legislation. His conclusions can be summarised as follows:

- custodial sentences in particular are meant to punish *and* deter
- such a sentence—in having to be commensurate with the seriousness of the offence—had to be commensurate with the punishment and deterrence which the seriousness of the offence required (*R v. Cunningham* (1993) 14 Cr App R(S) 386).

However, the Court of Appeal made it clear that increasing a sentence beyond the length which by those criteria is commensurate with seriousness to make an example of the defendant (sometimes called an 'exemplary sentence') offends the principle of proportionality.

Prevalence of offences

The fact that an offence is prevalent—locally or nationally—may make it more serious. A distinction must be drawn between the fact that an offence occurs frequently (which many offences do) and what might be termed 'a real outburst' of a particular type of offence and one that is perhaps gaining momentum. Court of Appeal guidance provides examples of ways in which the prevalence of a particular offence can increase its seriousness: e.g. a spate of public order offences can increase fear among residents generally in a given area and limit their freedom of movement. The decision as to what effect prevalence has on the seriousness of offences is ultimately one for the youth court in the light of all the circumstances.

Some other key principles

When making a sentence decision, the following recurring items should be borne in mind:

- the rule that the seriousness of the current offence may be assessed by looking at the current offence and one or more offences 'associated' with it. In broad terms, this means any other offences for which the juvenile is being sentenced at the same time (including offences which he or she is asking the youth court to take into consideration).

> All references in this handbook to the seriousness of an offence should be understood to mean of *the offence and any associated offences* which are relevant when assessing seriousness.

- the statutory rules whereby racially aggravated offences and offences committed whilst the offender is on bail must be treated as more serious by virtue of each of these facts
- the statutory obligation to consider giving credit for a guilty plea (because e.g. it is timely and avoids the need for witnesses to attend court and give evidence), when the youth court should reduce the penalty by possibly up to one third. If it does give credit it must state this fact in open court (and as a matter of practice ought to explain if it does not give credit).
- the totality principle which affects all sentencing decisions where there are a number of offences. The sentences, in combination, should not be out of all proportion to the nature of the offending under consideration. What this means in practice is that when imposing several sentences at the same time—particularly if they concern the same events—the youth court should review the total effect and make any appropriate downwards adjustment.
- the rule in section 29 Criminal Justice Act 1991 (as amended) under which previous findings of guilt and responses to earlier orders of the court can be taken into account when assessing the seriousness of the present offence or offences. In principle, analogous considerations apply where there has been an earlier police warning or reprimand (not yet universally in force: *Chapter 3*), although there is no statutory base to support this view. With convictions, warnings or reprimands, the question is always 'What is their relevance to sentence in the present case?'

A note on previous convictions and responses

So far as previous convictions are concerned, it is the practice of prosecutors in the youth court to submit lists of previous findings of guilt once a juvenile has pleaded guilty or has been found guilty by the court (*Chapter 6*). If a juvenile has a 'previous record' of offending, particularly for similar offences, this reduces the extent to which he or she can put forward mitigation on the ground of good character—and it may affect the youth court's view of a particular type of order. Similarly, if e.g. earlier community orders have not been complied with, this may indicate something about the suitability of such orders now. Section 29 states that in considering the seriousness of the offence:

> . . . the court may take into account any previous convictions of the offender or any failure of his to respond to previous sentences.

Clearly, a juvenile with no previous findings of guilt might claim that the offence was less serious because it, e.g. it stemmed from 'a foolish, youthful, immature, spur of the moment decision by someone with an otherwise unblemished record' (and possibly lacking in understanding of the consequences). Existing findings of guilt would, to the extent that they are relevant to the situation, limit or eradicate the scope for this.

It is less clear to what extent previous convictions can increase (or 'aggravate') the seriousness of the present offence—but, following basic principles, it seems clear that they ought not to be used to justify a sentence wholly *disproportionate* to that offence. It is similarly unclear how and to what extent failure to respond to previous sentences can affect the seriousness of the current offence, but this is something that the youth court must resolve in an individual case.

Identifying relevant convictions and failures

Commentators on section 29 have expressed concern that it is now easier for the courts to send minor offenders into custody—and it is doubly important for youth courts dealing with juvenile offenders to adopt a careful approach when assessing the relevance of any previous record to the seriousness of an offence.

Section 29 does not mean that all previous matters are capable of affecting the seriousness of an offence. The youth court should always consider the relevance of previous incidents and how they relate to the present situation. They should also be conscious about how much emphasis they place on the juvenile's record when deciding upon seriousness. As a matter of good practice, courts should clearly identify which convictions or failures are relevant for this purpose and then consider what the effect of such convictions or failures is in relation to seriousness. Even where previous findings of guilt or failures to respond to previous orders of the court do affect the seriousness of the offence the question 'To what extent?' must always be answered. For further guidance seek legal advice: 📖✍.

Court of Appeal and other guidance

Often, court legal advisers can offer guidance based on Court of Appeal rulings and inform the youth court of the approach which has been

adopted locally in any similar cases. The adviser should also
position to say what community provision for juveniles is avail.
locally in so far as this has features relevant to a case before the court.

II: WELFARE, JUST DESERTS AND PREVENTING CRIME

A main thrust of the Criminal Justice Act 1991 was the idea that the
sentence for an offence should relate primarily to—and be
commensurate with—the seriousness of the present offence and any
offences associated with it (see under *General Principles,* above). This
applies to offenders of all ages. It is thus the starting point in the youth
court, just as it is in the magistrates' court. However, there has to be
balanced against this another provision which affects all juvenile
offenders. The 'welfare principle' is contained in section 44 Children and
Young Persons Act 1933. It states that:

> Every court in dealing with a child or young person who is brought before
> it, either as an offender or otherwise, shall have regard to the welfare of the
> child or young person, and shall in a proper case take steps for removing
> him from undesirable surroundings, and for securing that proper provision
> is made for his education and training.

It is unfortunate that neither the Criminal Justice Act 1991 nor the
Children Act 1989 (with its emphasis on supporting children within their
families) explains how section 44 should be applied in the light of these
later provisions—so as to clarify its modern purpose. There is in fact no
statutory guidance on the interaction of the often competing welfare and
just deserts considerations and the youth court must itself decide what
weight to give to each in a given case and deal with any resulting
tensions. In practice, this is likely to be heavily influenced by the
assessment in any PSR (*Chapter 6*) or other information indicating that a
particular order has more potential in terms of the juvenile's welfare
than another.

Provisions which reinforce the 'welfare' approach
Other provisions are also relevant in relation to the welfare of juveniles:

- that part of Schedule 2 to the Children Act 1989 which obliges
  local authorities to take reasonable steps designed:
  —to reduce the need to bring criminal proceedings against
    children in their area
  —to encourage children in their area not to commit criminal
    offences

—to avoid the need for children in their area to be put into secure accommodation

- the new law on warnings and reprimands which involves diverting juvenile's who have committed criminal offences from the youth court process: *Chapter 3*
- requirements which oblige the Crown prosecutor to review prosecutions against juveniles in the context of special youth oriented criteria and to consider the possibility of a warning or reprimand even though the proceedings may have started and possibly have reached the youth court
- provisions of the Criminal Justice Act 1991 whereby, when making a community sentence, the court must select the order or orders which are 'most suitable for the offender': see, generally, *Section V* of this chapter
- the United Nations Convention on the Rights of the Child (1989) which requires that in all actions concerning people under 18 years of age before courts of law their best interests shall be the primary consideration.

Preventing offending

Indeed, Jack Straw, Home Secretary has indicated that preventing offending by juveniles promotes their welfare and protects the public. All youth justice agencies regularly perform the difficult task of reconciling welfare considerations of the kind outlined above with other potentially conflicting aims, not simply just deserts considerations. There is now a need to do the same vis-à-vis welfare and the new principal statutory aim of youth justice to prevent offending (p.13). It can be suggested that this means that crime prevention in relation to individual offenders needs to proceed gradually from a welfare base in the direction of prosecution, punishment and just deserts considerations, not simply vault in the direction of strong penal sanctions, possibly of a deterrent nature, and which, in any event, might risk exceeding what is required by a commensurate sentence. This latter approach would seem to be altogether at odds with welfare unless the argument is along dubious lines such as 'Punishment is good for you'. In other words, preventing offending implies an approach which acknowledges the good sense of strategies geared to solving the problems of youth crime through a juvenile's parents, guardians and local community, and—where the matter does come to court—through, e.g. community-based sentencing options which have prevention components to the fore in relevant programmes and schemes. Only when seriousness or the need to protect the public from the offender itself justifies a different, 'firmer' approach to preventing offending would it seem appropriate to see prevention in terms of punishment and the possible use of custody.

Correspondingly, the community-based agencies should see their work in the context of wider crime prevention strategies which need to be a central feature of the local authority's annual youth justice plan.

The need for a shared approach
When formally and universally in force, YOTs should automatically lead to better and more universally agreed strategies and approaches to juvenile crime, bringing together the elements of welfare, crime prevention and crime reduction. The youth court has always been a focus for the interaction of much related activity and the success of its own role has depended on a network of other people. Members of the youth court panel should be alert to the scope and extent of new and emerging services for juveniles, what facilities are available and the fact that YOTs will be at the hub of service delivery. Knowledge and awareness of how YOTs work and what they achieve in terms of dealing with offenders will directly affect whether the correct orders are made.

III: PARENTAL RESPONSIBILITY

The trend is towards encouraging greater involvement by parents or guardians in all aspects of youth justice—albeit that many juvenile offenders come from difficult family backgrounds where the juvenile's offending might add to existing tensions in an already fragile situation. Efforts to involve parents and guardians have a long history:

> Crime prevention begins in the home. Parents have the most influence on their children's development. From their children's earliest years, parents can and should help them develop as responsible law abiding citizens. They should ensure that their children are aware of the existence of rules and laws, and the need for them; and that they respect other people and their property . . . when young people offend, the law has a part to play in reminding parents of their responsibilities. (From the White Paper, *Crime, Justice and Protecting the Public* (1990)).

The Criminal Justice Act 1991 drew a distinction between offenders under the age of 16 years—in respect of whom parental responsibility is a presumption—and those aged 16 and 17—when the presumption is to the opposite effect, i.e. that the juvenile is responsible for his or her own behaviour unless the facts of an individual case show otherwise. In other words, there is a gradual diminution in parental responsibility in relation to 16 and 17-year-olds to take account of the maturity of the offender.

Attendance at court of parents or guardian
In the case of an offender under 16, the court *must* require parents or guardians to attend court during all stages of the proceedings unless satisfied that it would be unreasonable to do so. Where the offender is

aged 16 or 17, the court *may* require the parents or guardians to attend: see *Chapter 6* for parents etc. taking part in relevant court procedures.

RESPONSIBILITY FOR FINANCIAL PENALTIES

Where the court imposes a fine, compensation or costs, and the offender is under 16, it *must* order the parent or guardian to pay the financial penalty unless this would be unreasonable in the circumstances, or the parent or guardian cannot be found. If the offender is 16 or 17-years-old the court *may* order the parent or guardian to pay.

Parent's or guardian's opportunity to make representations
No such financial order can be made without first giving the parent or guardian an opportunity to be heard. If he or she fails to attend court an order may only be made where there has been a requirement to attend, notice of this has been served, and the parent or guardian has failed to do so. The parent or guardian can appeal in his or her own right against any financial order made as a result.

Relevant considerations
In deciding whether to require parents or guardians to pay financial penalties, consideration needs to be given to matters such as whether they have neglected to exercise proper care and control of the juvenile, and whether such neglect has, in some way, caused or contributed to the offence. Other relevant considerations might include whether, in the circumstances, it is proper for the juvenile to assume responsibility for payment (many juveniles have income from part-time or full-time employment); whether they are otherwise 'self-sufficient'; the nature of the relationship between the juvenile and the parent or guardian—and the likely effect on that relationship of any order. Finally, the means of the juvenile and the parent or guardian need to be considered by the court.

Where the parent or guardian *is* ordered to pay, then the amount of any financial order (usually fines or compensation) has to be fixed in accordance with the financial circumstances of the parent or guardian and not those of the juvenile offender.

Local authorities
In relation to a juvenile for whom a local authority has parental responsibility—and who is either in their care or accommodated by them—the local authority will be deemed to be the parent or guardian for the purposes of financial penalties. However, the responsibility here is simply for payment. In deciding the amount of the order the means of the local authority are irrelevant.

In 1995, the High Court considered the circumstances in which a court should make a compensation order against a local authority in respect of a juvenile found guilty of a criminal offence. It was argued that if the court was satisfied that the local authority had done all that could be expected of it, in caring for the child or young person, it would be unreasonable to make such an order. A two stage approach applies. Firstly, the court should consider whether a compensation order was right in principle, i.e. had a victim suffered loss which deserved to be compensated? The second stage was for the youth court to determine whether the local authority should be made responsible for compensation. Where the local authority was found to have done everything which it reasonably and properly could to protect the public from the criminal actions of the juvenile offender, it was 'wholly unreasonable and unjust' for that authority to bear a financial penalty. This would place the local authority in a position worse than that of a natural parent. The High Court went on to say that where a local authority wished to counter suggestions that it should pay compensation, then it should be ready to call evidence as to the manner in which it had acted. Clearly, the youth court should be ready and willing to grant any necessary adjournment to allow this to happen.

BINDING OVER PARENTS OR GUARDIANS

The court can order parents or guardians to enter into a recognisance to take proper care or exercise proper control over the juvenile. The parent or guardian must consent to any such order, but where consent is unreasonably refused the court has power to fine the parent or guardian up to £1,000. Any recognisance which is forfeited is enforceable as a fine.

Where the juvenile is under 16 years of age, the court *must* exercise its power to bind over the parent or guardian if it is satisfied that it is desirable to do so in the interests of preventing the commission of further offences. Reasons must be given by the court for not exercising the power to bind them over.

In respect of juveniles aged 16 and 17, the duty to bind over parents is replaced by a discretion—i.e. a parent or guardian *may* be bound over.

Factors affecting decisions whether to bind over a parent or guardian are likely to reflect those described in relation to financial penalties above—but it must be remembered that it is legitimate to use this power only if there has been a failure to exercise proper care and control.

Amount and period of bind over
The amount of the 'parental recognisance' may not exceed £1,000. The means of the parent or guardian must be taken into account when setting the amount—which may be increased or decreased in line with those

means. The order may be for a period not exceeding three years, or until the juvenile reaches the age of 18, whichever is the shorter. It can be varied or revoked on application, if it appears to the court, having regard to any change of circumstances since the order was made, that this would be in the interests of justice.

Local authorities
Where the local authority has parental responsibility there is no power to bind over either the authority or its representative.

Binding over and community orders
Since 1995, courts have had power to add a condition to a parental bind over requiring the parent or guardian to ensure that the juvenile complies with any community order imposed on the juvenile. This might be used, e.g. when the court thinks that it is appropriate that a parent or guardian should take steps to ensure that the juvenile attends at an attendance centre, turns up for community service or keeps an appointment with a supervisor (see, generally, *Section V* of this chapter).

Again, factors affecting a decision whether to bind over a parent or guardian are likely to reflect the 'maturity' considerations described in relation to financial penalties above. In addition, the court should have in mind compliance by the juvenile with the community order.

A local authority or a representative thereof cannot be bound over.

Appeals
A parent, guardian or local authority may appeal against any financial penalty which they are ordered to pay. Furthermore, a parent or guardian may appeal against a parental bind over.

Parental bind over—forfeiture of recognisance
There is uncertainty whether jurisdiction to deal with the forfeiture of a parental recognisance lies with the ordinary magistrates' court or the youth court and about who can bring proceedings. In answer to a 'Practical Point' submitted by a reader, *Justice of the Peace* journal concluded that jurisdiction may lie with either court (160 JPN 468). The Justices' Clerks' Society has expressed a similar view: generally 📖✋.

PARENTING ORDERS

The Crime and Disorder Act 1998 introduced this new order (not yet universally in force) with the object of encouraging parents to accept more responsibility for the behaviour of their children. The parenting order will offer parents training and help to change the offending behaviour of their children and contain a requirement that they exercise control over their children's behaviour. The youth court must be satisfied that the order would be desirable in the interests of preventing the commission of further offences.

A parenting order can come about in a number of ways but in the youth court it will arise mainly when a child aged ten to 17 is being sentenced by the youth court for a criminal offence.

The requirements of the order will be supervised by a responsible officer who will either be a social worker, a probation officer or a member of a YOT: *Chapter 2.*

The parenting order is applicable to parents or guardians. This includes someone who, though not a parent, has parental responsibility or who has care of the child. It may be made in respect of one or both parents—this being a matter for the court to decide in the circumstances of an individual case. The court will need to satisfy itself that the parent or guardian is in fact in a position to help and support the child.

Before making a parenting order, the court must obtain information about the family circumstances and the likely affect of the order on those circumstances. This does not mean there has to be a written report, but in practice there will be one.

What a parenting order involves

The order will require the parents etc. to attend training and guidance sessions and/or to comply with other requirements intended to ensure that they take proper care of the child. It may be made for a period not exceeding three months but attendance at guidance or training sessions cannot be for more than one session per week. Requirements to exercise control can last for up to 12 months. An example of control requirements placed on parents might be that they ensure that the child is at home between certain hours, or that he or she is escorted to and from school by a responsible adult.

The court imposing the order does not have to seek the parents' or guardians' consent, but it will be prudent for the youth court to ensure that there will be cooperation by them. Before making a parenting order, it must explain to the parent or guardian, in ordinary language:

- the effect of the order and of the requirements proposed to be included in it;
- the consequences which may follow if he or she fails to comply with any of the requirements; and
- that the court has the power to review the order on the application of the parent or guardian or responsible officer.

Should the parent or guardian fail to comply with any of the requirements of a parenting order without reasonable excuse, he or she will be liable to a fine not exceeding Level 3 on the standard scale (at present up to £1000), or the court may impose any other sentence which is available for non-imprisonable offences.

Piloting
The parenting order is one of many measures under the Crime and Disorder Act 1998 which are being piloted in test areas. The pilot schemes run for 18 months from the autumn of 1998.

Duty to notify courts of arrangements
In making this ancillary order, the court must have been notified that arrangements exist in the area in which the parent or guardian lives.

Appeal
Appeal is possible, and this will normally be to the Crown Court.

IV: FOUR LEVELS OF SENTENCE

The four basic levels of sentence—within which a specially adapted scheme of orders for people in the youth court age group operates (see *Powers of the youth court*, below)—are as follows:

- **DISCHARGES**: punishment is 'inexpedient'.
- **FINES**: by implication punishment *is* expedient (but more severe punishment is inappropriate). The size of a fine must reflect the seriousness of the offence and take into account the financial circumstances of the juvenile (or his or her parent or guardian).
- **COMMUNITY SENTENCES**: the offence is 'serious enough'. The degree of 'restriction of liberty' must be commensurate with the seriousness of the offence.
- **CUSTODY**:
  —the offence is so serious that *only* such a sentence can be justified; or
  —if the offence is a sexual or violent offence (pp.136-137), only such a sentence would be adequate to protect the public from serious harm from the offender; or
  —the offender has refused to consent to a community sentence proposed by the court and which requires that consent. Custody is also possible on breach of some community sentences where there has been 'wilful and persistent' failure to comply with such a sentence.

Length of custodial sentences
The *length* of a custodial sentence must be commensurate with the seriousness of the offence. However, there is—in the case of a sexual or

violent offence—power to pass a longer than commensurate sentence (as there is in the case of an adult) where this is necessary to protect the public from serious harm from the offender.

Seriousness of the offence

As indicated earlier in this chapter, in the vast majority of cases in the youth court the seriousness of the offence determines which of the four levels of sentence should be considered and the extent of any penalty. Any number of associated offences can be taken into account when assessing seriousness: see *Part I* of this chapter, *General Considerations*.

Powers of the youth court

The youth court's full range of powers to make orders following a plea of guilty or a finding of guilt are set out in detail in *Section V* of this chapter and in *Chart 5, Sentences Available in the Youth Court* in *Part III* of the handbook. The main differences between the powers of the adult court and the youth court can be summarised:

- *Discharges*
  The youth court's powers to order absolute or conditional discharges are the same as those of the adult court except that the latter cannot normally be imposed within two years of a police warning: *Chapter 3.*

- *Fines*
  The same general criteria for fines apply subject to special ceilings:
  — in the case of a child (10 to 13 years inclusive) £250;
  — in the case of a young person (14 to 17 years inclusive) £1,000.

* Parents or guardians *can*—in some instances *must*—be ordered to pay fines imposed on their children. The upper child and young offender ceilings still apply: *Parental Responsibility*, above.

- *Compensation*
  In contrast to the special lower ceilings for fines, the upper limit for compensation in the youth court is the same as that in the adult court, namely £5,000 per offence.

* Parents or guardians *can*—in some instances *must*—be ordered to pay compensation for their children: *Parental Responsibility*, above.

- *Community sentences*
  Probation orders, community service orders, combination orders and curfew orders are available in the youth court—but only for people aged 16 years and over.

A different species of community sentence—the supervision order—can be made for up to three years in respect of juveniles up to and including 17 years of age. The supervisor may be a local authority social worker or a probation officer.

Attendance centre orders are available for a hybrid group of juveniles and other young offenders within the age group 10 to 20 years (with special attendance limits for younger offenders).

Action plan orders can only be made in respect of juveniles.

- *Custody*
Juveniles, whether male or female, aged 15 to 17 inclusive can be sentenced to detention in a young offender institution (YOI) run by the Prison Service. For this age group, there is a special minimum sentence of two months (thereby ensuring that custody must really be called for). The maximum is six months per offence in the youth court; or 12 months in aggregate where there are two or more indictable offences. The maximum in the Crown Court is two years per offence (see under *Committal for Sentence* on p.144-145) except in the somewhat special case of grave crimes, below:

Juveniles aged 12 to 14-years inclusive are eligible for *Secure Training Orders:* see pp.141-142.

Long-term detention for homicide and certain other offences can be ordered by the Crown Court if the youth court sends the case there at the outset: see *Grave Crimes*, pp.55-59 and, generally, seek advice 📖✋.

The detention and training order introduced by the Crime and Disorder Act 1998 (not yet in force) can range in length from four months to two years.

NB: There is no such thing as a suspended sentence in the youth court or in relation to a juvenile offender.

No separate penalty

The non-statutory device of 'no separate penalty' (or NSP) is used by many courts, usually where there is a significant number of findings of guilt and orders made in relation to the more serious matters are considered sufficient to reflect the totality of the offending on a given occasion. Typically, the offences will be of a relatively minor nature and not affect other aspects of the court's decision. NSP and endorsement of a driving licence for the same offence is not uncommon: 📖✋.

V: SENTENCES AND ORDERS

This section outlines each of the powers of the youth
attention to areas where these depart from those of the
descriptions are intended to be read in conjunction wit
III, Sentences Available in the Youth Court. General c
relation to juvenile offenders described in other earlier sections must
always be borne in mind—particularly age, welfare and preventing
offences.

Discharges

> **CRITERION**: '. . . having regard to the circumstances including
> the nature of the offence and the character of the offender . . . it is
> inexpedient to inflict punishment . . .'

> **RESTRICTION ON LIBERTY**: none implied or arising.

> **SPECIAL CONSIDERATIONS FOR JUVENILE OFFENDERS:**
> None: other than the general one that periods of time may seem
> longer to a juvenile than they do to an adult, so that e.g.
> depending on the age of the juvenile, a conditional discharge for,
> say, two or three years may seem to be for an endless and
> possibly 'meaningless' period of time.

Absolute discharge
This marks the conviction but no other obligations follow. An absolute
discharge may be appropriate when the offence is of a truly minor
nature, purely technical, or when there are several offences and a
comparatively trivial one requires a residual sentencing disposal (which
might equally be achieved by imposing 'no separate penalty': see *Section
IV* of this chapter).

Conditional discharge
This makes the offender subject to a single condition, i.e. that no further
offence is committed within a period of up to three years—as determined
by the court and usually called 'the operational period'. Conviction of
any criminal offence during the operational period renders the offender
liable to be re-sentenced for the offence which originally gave rise to the
conditional discharge—over and above any sentence for the new offence.

.urt must explain the effects of the conditional discharge to the
.1der.

Unlike a probation order or supervision order, a conditional
discharge involves no monitoring or follow up of the juvenile's
behaviour during the period of the discharge.

Conditional discharge and the Crime and Disorder Act 1998

The 1998 Act contains provisions concerning warnings and reprimands
which are being piloted in specific areas for 18 months from 30
September 1998, leading to national implementation during 2000/2001:
see *Chapter 3*. The use of conditional discharges for young offenders who
have previously received warnings is restricted. Unless there are
exceptional circumstances relating directly to the offence or offender, a
conditional discharge cannot be imposed for a crime committed within
two years of receiving a warning. Courts which do find exceptional
circumstances must explain their reasons when making a conditional
discharge in such circumstances.

Similarly, where someone is found guilty of a breach of an anti-social
behaviour order (p.155) or of a sex offender order (p.156), the court is
precluded from imposing a conditional discharge for that breach.

Breach of conditional discharge

A breach occurs if a fresh criminal offence is committed during the
operational period. When the court comes to re-sentence the offender for
the original offence, the seriousness of that offence has to be considered
afresh. Apart from substituting a different disposal, the court has the
option of taking no action and allowing the conditional discharge to run
if it thinks this is the proper course. Subject to any rules about
considering the remittal of a juvenile offender to the youth court for his
or her own area after a finding of guilt or a plea of guilty, breach of a
conditional discharge imposed by a youth court can be dealt with
anywhere in England and Wales (subject to the consent of the original
court if in a different place).

Fines

> CRITERION: this is not directly covered by any statute. By
> implication, fines should be used where a discharge is not
> appropriate, i.e. where punishment *is* expedient—but a more
> severe sentence would not be. The *size* of a fine must reflect the
> seriousness of the offence and take into account the offender's (or
> parent's or guardian's) financial circumstances.

> **RESTRICTION ON LIBERTY**: fines do not affect the physical liberty of the offender, but a loss of spending power deprives the offender of the ability to direct money towards recreation and leisure, or to choose how he or she spends a sum of money equivalent to the amount of the fine.

> **SPECIAL CONSIDERATIONS FOR JUVENILE OFFENDERS**: There are special maximum limits (set out below) and the youth court must consider whether the parent or guardian should be ordered to pay the fine following the special rules for different age groups described under *Parental Responsibility* in *Section III* of this chapter.

The maximum fine in the youth court (whether ordered to be paid by the juvenile or the parent, guardian, etc.) is:

- £250 in the case of a child (i.e. ten to 13 inclusive)
- £1,000 in the case of a young person (14 to 17 inclusive).

This maximum reduces if the adult maximum is lower, i.e. the maximum fine for a Level 1 offence is £200, Level 2 £500. (Other adult fine levels are above the juvenile maxima). All figures are given as at January 1999. These are uprated by Parliament from time to time, the last time in 1992.

Fixing the amount of the fine
This involves the court in the following tasks:

- an inquiry into the 'financial circumstances' of the offender (or his or her parent or guardian as the case may be: see *Parental Responsibility*)
- taking these into account (so far as they are known or appear)
- reflecting the seriousness of the offence
- taking all other relevant circumstances into account.

Financial circumstances
Courts can increase or decrease the size of a fine according to an individual juvenile's financial circumstances (or his or her parent's or guardian's financial circumstances as the case may be). If there are several fines (and/or *Compensation to Victims* or *Costs*: see later in this chapter) the court must bear in mind the total impact on the offender's (parent's etc) finances and may need to adjust the time for payment.

The term 'financial circumstances' is wide in scope. It probably covers not only direct income but also, e.g. savings, investments, endowment policies and any valuable possessions, as well as permitting a court to consider the position of, say, an offender with no apparent income but who is living a fairly lavish lifestyle, based possibly on a partner's support. This last point is yet to be tested in the higher courts. The pre-1991 law was against, e.g. family income being considered.

Financial penalties should usually be set at a level which envisages payment within 12 months or possibly less if the juvenile is ordered to pay in person. It is suggested by the authors of this handbook that the adult rule whereby *some* financial orders may properly be ordered to be paid over up to two or even three years only applies in practice in exceptional situations (e.g. where the offender has very significant means or prospects). This gloss on the basic rule of 'no longer than 12 months' should therefore be viewed with extra caution in the case of a juvenile for whom an 'unimaginably long' commitment may prove counter-productive. It *might* be more appropriate to extend the period of 12 months where loss to a victim is involved and compensation is ordered—although even here caution is needed in the case of an order against a juvenile. There may be more room for manoeuvre where a parent or guardian is made to pay as it is his or her financial circumstances which become relevant: *Section IV*, *Parental Responsibility*.

Financial circumstances orders
After conviction but *before* sentence, a defendant can be made subject to a 'financial circumstances order' (or *before* conviction if he or she has written pleading guilty under the procedure for *Written Pleas of Guilty: Chapter 2*). The defendant is then required to provide such a statement of his or her financial circumstances as the court may require. This may be by way of written details or in answer to inquiries in court. Failure to comply is an offence punishable by a Level 3 fine (£1,000). False or incomplete disclosure is a separate offence carrying three months' imprisonment and/or a Level 4 fine (£2,500). The same applies to the parent or guardian.

Combining fines with other sentences
Caution is necessary before ordering more than one penalty for a single offence, especially in the case of a juvenile—if only because the resulting 'restriction of liberty' may be disproportionate to the offence given the age, maturity and welfare of the offender. However, legally speaking, fines *are* capable of being imposed in addition to custody. Some courts take the view that a fine and a community sentence cannot be imposed for a single offence, or that this would be inappropriate (see also p.119). Unless and until this is resolved by a binding legal ruling magistrates should check what view is taken locally: 📖✋ .

The possibility of a fine and a discharge for a single offence can hardly arise given the criterion for discharges (i.e. 'punishment is inexpedient', above). Ancillary orders can always be added to a fine: see sections *VI, Compensation* and *VII, Other Orders of the Youth Court.*

A compensation order can be made in its own right or can be combined with any other sentence.

If both a fine and compensation are considered appropriate and the juvenile or his or her parent or guardian cannot realistically be ordered to pay both in full because of their financial circumstances, then the compensation order must always be preferred at the expense of the fine (and by implication any prosecution costs).

Excise penalties

Certain convictions result in an 'excise penalty' rather than a fine, such as keeping an untaxed vehicle and certain Customs and Excise offences. Generally speaking, such penalties are collected and enforced in the same way as fines (further advice should be sought as necessary: 📖).

Payment and collection of fines

Fines, compensation and costs are due and payable forthwith unless the court orders otherwise—and offenders cannot automatically expect weekly or other 'easy terms'. Where appropriate, payment can be allowed by a fixed date or by instalments. Payment can always be made in cash and by various other methods: postal order, cheque (bank giro, credit card or transcash if individual courts accept these methods).

Remission and alteration of fines

A later court has power to remit a fine, in whole or in part, in the light of any subsequent change in circumstances. This will often be in enforcement proceedings. A separate power allows a later court to remit all or part of a fine where it was originally fixed in the offender's absence—which is relatively unusual in the case of a juvenile although this can now happen where the procedure for *Written Pleas of Guilty* is invoked—or without an adequate statement of financial circumstances where information before the later court suggests that, had the original court had such information, it would have fixed a lower fine or no fine at all. A compensation order cannot be remitted, but can be discharged or reduced by a later court in limited circumstances: seek advice: 📖 .

Immediate enforcement

The following measures apply to all types of financial order:

Power to search

On imposing the fine (or e.g. in enforcement proceedings) magistrates can order the payer/defaulter to be searched—usually by a police officer or gaoler—and any monies found can be applied to meeting sums due. Regard must be had to domestic needs.

Immediate custody

Juveniles cannot be sent to custody for default. There are three circumstances in which magistrates can order a parent or guardian to be imprisoned in default if they have been ordered to pay:

- where the offence is imprisonable in the case of an adult and the parent/guardian appears to have the means to pay forthwith (which might include withdrawing money from a savings account)
- where it appears that the parent/guardian is unlikely to remain long enough at a place of abode in the UK to enforce the fine by other means (e.g. a person of no fixed abode or who is about to go abroad)
- the parent/guardian is already serving a prison sentence.

Custody in default may be suspended on terms at the time of imposing a fine (where permissible: above) or at the enforcement stage.

General enforcement powers

In all other circumstances the full enforcement process applies and a subsequent enquiry must be held into the default. On imposing financial penalties courts can set a review hearing date when enforcement will be considered if payment has not been made. Once the defaulter is before the court (which he or she normally must be), there are various enforcement options. These are not dealt with in detail in this handbook and advice should be taken locally (📖✎), especially if custody in default (i.e. of the parent or guardian) is in prospect. In summary, the court can:

- set further terms for payment
- search the juvenile or his or her parents or guardians
- make an attachment of earnings order (i.e. to an employer)
- ask the Benefits Agency to deduct the fine from income support
- issue a distress warrant to seize the defaulter's goods (which may be immediate or suspended on terms)
- in the case of a juvenile, make an attendance centre order
- in the case of a juvenile, transfer the fine to the parent or guardian: p.113
- make a money payment supervision order (usually operated by the Probation Service or a court civilian enforcement officer
- order a defaulter *who is 18 years of age or over* (some juveniles will have attained the age of 18 by this stage) to be detained:
  — in the court precincts or a police station until 8 pm
  —overnight in a police station

—in a young offender institution or in the case of a parent or guardian in a prison within a scale which relates maximum periods to amounts outstanding. Either type of order can be suspended on terms.

- apply to the High Court or county court for civil remedies
- remit or alter the fine (see *Remission and alteration of fines,* above).

Venue for the enforcement proceedings

Where a juvenile is ordered to pay and enforcement becomes necessary this will be heard in the youth court (possibly in the adult court if he or she has now turned 18). If the parent or guardian is responsible and enforcement becomes necessary, this will be heard in the adult court. The adult court may consider making an order that the identity of the juvenile is not revealed in any press report or publication.

Order against parent or guardian to pay

The parent's or guardian's position is outlined under *Financial Responsibility,* above. Considerations of responsibility do not just apply at the time of sentence. Where the juvenile was originally ordered to pay, the court may later order the parent or guardian to do so if it is satisfied that the juvenile defaulter has, or has had since the date the sum was imposed, the means to pay and is now refusing or neglecting to pay (or has refused or neglected to pay) and for want of distress. There must be reasonable grounds for making this order against the parent, who must be given the opportunity to make representations. If the order is made the effect is that the parent takes over payment and the financial order then becomes enforceable against him or her in the adult court.

Binding over parents or guardians to ensure that the juvenile pays

This can be considered where the court is satisfied that the defaulter has, or has had since the date when the sum was ordered, the means to pay the sum or any instalment on which he or she has defaulted, and refuses or neglects (or has refused or neglected) to pay and for want of distress. The court has a discretion to require the juvenile's parent of guardian to enter into a recognisance (subject to consent) to ensure that the juvenile pays the outstanding sum. Ultimate responsibility for payment still rests with the juvenile in these circumstances.

Community Sentences

> **THRESHOLD CRITERION**: '. . . the offence, or the combination of the offence and one or more offences associated with it, [is] serious enough to warrant such a sentence'. This applies to *all* eight community orders below. The *serious enough* threshold must be reached *before* a particular order or orders can be chosen.

> **RESTRICTION ON LIBERTY**: all community sentences place demands on the offender's time, energies or activities. The extent of the restriction must be ' . . . commensurate with the seriousness of the offence, or the combination of the offence and one or more offences associated with it': see also *Special Considerations For Juveniles*, below.

> **SUITABILITY**: There is an extra (and sometimes conflicting consideration) in that the community order or orders selected must be the most suitable for the offender: below.

> **SPECIAL CONSIDERATIONS FOR JUVENILES**: The availability of some community orders depends on age limits. Special attention must also be given to the existence of the supervision order (and the choice which this gives to youth courts between probation orders and supervision orders for 16 and 17-year-olds).
>
> When considering the extent of the restriction of liberty imposed by a given community order, the youth court will need to take account of this in the light of the age, maturity etc. of the individual juvenile. In some instances, what might have seemed manageable in the case of an adult may be daunting and counter-productive in the case of a juvenile.
>
> Parents or guardians (but not local authorities) can be bound over to ensure compliance with a community sentence; parents or guardians may also be the subject of parenting orders: see *Section III* of this chapter, *Parental Responsibility*.

Associated offences
Associated offences has the meaning set out in *Section I* of this chapter.

The eight community orders

A community sentence is ' . . . a sentence which consists of or includes one or more community orders . . . '. This enables courts to tailor individual decisions by selecting one or more orders from the menu of eight community orders, even theoretically for a single offence: but see *Combining community sentences* and *Chart V* in *Part III* of this handbook. So far as juveniles are concerned the eight orders are as follows:

- action plan order*
- drug treatment and testing order*
- supervision order (with or without added requirements)
- probation order (with or without added requirements): 16 and 17 year olds only
- community service order: 16 and 17 year olds only
- combination order: 16 and 17 year olds only
- curfew order: 16 and 17 year olds only*
- attendance centre order ('junior centre'): age 10 to 17.
(* When and where in force: see sections on individual orders)

Restriction on liberty and suitability

Once the court is satisfied that the offence or offences are 'serious enough' to warrant a community sentence, two main considerations arise:

- the community order (or orders) must be the 'most suitable for the offender'
- the restriction on liberty arising from the community order (or orders) must be commensurate with the seriousness of the offence or offences.

There is thus a dual responsibility for the sentencer: that of deciding on the appropriate degree of *restriction on liberty* (as determined by the seriousness of the offence or offences), whilst ensuring that the community order or orders is or are *the most suitable for the offender*. This balancing exercise makes considerable demands on sentencer's skills, and requires close attention if fair, appropriate and consistent sentencing practices are to be maintained. The statutory provision which creates these considerations mentions suitability *before* restriction on liberty. This is the only clue as to how any conflict might be resolved, i.e. possibly in favour of suitability (provided a 'suitable' sentence would not involve greater restriction of liberty than can be justified by the seriousness of the offence). In the case of juvenile offenders, these considerations also become intermingled with the welfare approach and the principle of preventing offending: *Section II* of this chapter.

Core issues

Sentencers need an understanding of certain core matters:

- the factors inherent in each type of offence which are likely to affect seriousness, whether as aggravating or mitigating factors
- any personal and other factors which may be relevant to seriousness (e.g. previous convictions, or in some instances the juvenile's own circumstances)
- what value to place on each of these factors so as to ensure a fair and consistent approach—taking account of good sentencing practice and local guidelines
- what each type of community order seeks to achieve and what demands it makes on a juvenile offender
- the comparative restriction on liberty which each of the six community orders places on the juvenile's liberty—and how these restrictions correlate in terms of duration, intensity, frequency and effect on juveniles.

Liaison

There is a need for dialogue between sentencers, local authority social services departments, probation officers and YOTs as appropriate—especially with those who write pre-sentence reports (*Chapters 2* and *6*) and who supervise community orders. There should be a clear understanding of the type and range of provision available locally and the aims, objectives and performance of particular programmes or schemes. Many youth courts have entered into liaison arrangements to ensure:

- a common understanding about the relationship between levels of seriousness and the restrictions on liberty which arises from particular community orders
- the provision of precise information about:
  —the content of community orders and the level of contact with offenders subject to them
  —sentencing outcomes, i.e. a periodic statement, in general terms, of the perceived success or otherwise of orders made by the court.

Factors relevant to seriousness

The same general factors affecting the assessment of seriousness apply in relation to community sentences as they do to other forms of sentence.

Some factors relevant to 'suitability'
The following may be particularly relevant to the *suitability* of an order
or orders for an individual offender.

—the type of restriction on liberty and effort or input required
—family, work, school or education commitments
—health issues
—the age, maturity and intellectual capabilities of the offender
—the offender's mobility or lack of it
—the perceived cause of offending
—the offender's own needs to enable him or her to turn away from
   offending
—the offender's general ability and motivation to undertake and
   complete the order
—the offender's consent and his or her willingness to comply with
   the order (which may be a statutory requirement: below)
—any risk of re-offending
—the protection of the public
—the prevention of future offending by the offender
—any responses to previous orders by the offender and especially
   community orders. Given the range and flexibility of community
   orders, failure to respond to one style of order may not be decisive
   if a proposed community sentence (such as probation or
   supervision) can be constructed so as to overcome previous
   difficulties.

Choice of order where the offender is 16 or 17
Apart from assessing the situation with such factors in mind, offending
by people aged 16 or 17 years needs to be considered with the choice
between probation supervision (16 to 17 year olds only) and a
supervision order to the local authority (10 to 17) in mind. However,
with the creation of multi-agency YOTs the distinction may be less
significant than before in those cases where powers overlap. The correct
approach/solution should be clear from the PSR produced by a member
of the YOT and it is unlikely that any particular order will need to be
made to 'spring' resources as might have sometimes been the case in the
past. Where in doubt about what order to make the court can consult the
writer of the PSR or his or her representative in court—and whilst it
should always bear in mind any agreed strategies (particularly where the
youth court has been a party to discussions) it is not bound by these if
the justice of the case dictates that there should be some other outcome.

Maturity
As indicated above, the court's assessment of the juvenile's maturity and
his or her consequent responsibility should be one factor in deciding

upon the appropriate type of order. Some commonly applied guideline indicators on 'maturity' may be of assistance. Depending on the circumstances of the case, local 'understandings' and the type of provision available from a particular agency, some of these factors may also assist the choice between probation and local authority supervision:

- *Some factors pointing to 'lack of maturity'*
—still dependent on parents or guardians in many respects
—even if theoretically financially independent, nevertheless irresponsible with finances
—still at school, or behind with schooling or a generally 'slow developer'
—unable or unwilling to engage in educational and other opportunities
—emotional mood swings associated with adolescence
—forms brief, transitory or inappropriate relationships
—unable to appreciate the victim's perspective
—unable to learn from experience, especially from consequences of offending
—unplanned, spur of the moment or thoughtless offence indicative of a failure to appreciate either its significance or the fact that it has led to court proceedings.

- *Some factors pointing to 'maturity'*
—ready, or planning for, independent living or already so living
—has some degree of financial independence and/or responsibility
—in some form of paid employment or a training scheme
—in some form of further or higher education
—aware of and capable of meeting emotional needs of self/others
—has experienced some close, meaningful relationships
—appreciation, or some appreciation, of the significance of the offence and the reason for the court proceedings, and of the victim's perspective
—able to learn from his or her experiences
—strong element of planning in offending.

Combining community orders

A community sentence may contain (subject to limitations) one or more of the eight community orders. The limitations are: probation and community service can only be combined by way of a combination order (below); community service cannot be combined with supervision (p.131); an action plan order cannot be combined with a custodial sentence, probation, community service, a combination order, supervision order or attendance centre order (p.120). Generally speaking advice should be sought if considering combining orders:📖✋.

The extent to which this facility to combine orders might be exercised seems not to have troubled youth courts which appear, on the whole, to have adhered to the previous practice whereby there could be only one distinct disposal for each offence. In constructing a community sentence containing multiple orders the court must consider the overall restriction of liberty and be careful not to arrive at a *disproportionate* sentence. Given that juvenile offenders may experience orders in a more onerous way to adults—in terms of length/quantum or content—a youth court should be doubly careful about overloading an offender or making the total restriction on liberty wholly disproportionate to the seriousness of the offence. Legal advice may be desirable: 📖✋.

Opinions appear to differ about imposing a fine and a community sentence for a single offence (see p.110)—although clearly a possibility in relation to separate offences even if dealt with on the same occasion.

Given the 'maturity' considerations which are likely to precipitate a supervision order to a local authority, it would seem hard, on the same occasion, to justify combining a different order for a separate offence.

Ancillary orders such as compensation, costs, endorsement and disqualification can always (and sometimes must: 📖✋) be added to a community sentence. Compensation must be considered in appropriate cases: see *Section VI* of this chapter.

PSRs and suitability

The need for sound information upon which to base a sentencing decision was highlighted in *Chapter 6*. In considering the question of suitability, the court must take into account any information before it about the offender. The court must normally obtain and consider a PSR *before* deciding on the suitability for the offender of certain orders:

- a probation order with added requirements
- a community service order
- a combination order
- a supervision order with special requirements
- a drug treatment and testing order.

The youth court can deem such a report to be 'unnecessary', but only if an earlier report (or the latest of several such reports) is available, which it then considers. Juveniles' lives can change rapidly, and good practice indicates that a fresh report should be obtained wherever possible. Foregoing a new or previous PSR will not, of itself, render an order invalid, but a PSR will usually have to be obtained if there is an appeal.

Consents and explanations

The youth court must explain to the juvenile and his or her parent or guardian the way in which it intends to deal with the juvenile and allow representations: *Chapter 6, Procedures, Information and Evidence.* Additionally, there is, in respect of most community orders, an independent obligation to explain to the offender the effect of the proposed order. This is good practice in any event. Under the Crime (Sentences) Act 1997, the need for offenders to consent to, or express a willingness to comply with, community orders was largely dispensed with. Such 'agreement' is now only required in relation to probation orders with additional requirements relating to treatment for a mental condition or drug/alcohol dependency and in respect of the new drug treatment and testing orders.

In respect of all community orders it is still essential to ensure that both the juvenile and his parents or guardians understand what is being proposed.

In those few instances where consent *is* needed, a refusal enables the court to consider custody (assuming the offence is imprisonable in the case of an adult). This is so, even if the particular offence was not deemed serious enough for custody in the first place. Custody can also be used on 'wilful and persistent' breach of the order provided the offence is imprisonable: see *Breach of Community Orders,* below.

Action Plan Orders

The action plan order is a novel form of community sentence introduced by the Crime and Disorder Act 1998 and is to be phased in: see *Pilot schemes,* below and ▢✍. It is specifically tailored to addressing the cause of a child or young person's offending behaviour. The court can make an action plan order when it considers that to do so will prevent re-offending or rehabilitate the offender. It is designed to provide a short but intensive and individually tailored response to offending behaviour, so that the causes of that offending as well as the offending itself, can be addressed. It cannot be combined with a custodial sentence, probation order, community service order, combination order, supervision order or attendance centre order.

The order places certain requirements on the juvenile which are supervised by a responsible officer. The offender is obliged to comply with a three month action plan.

Since the action plan order is a community sentence, the court must be satisfied that the offence, or the combination of the offence and other offences associated with it, is *serious enough* to warrant a community sentence. The intention of the government was that it should be used for relatively serious offending, but the order also represents an early opportunity for targeted intervention to help prevent further offending. Where the conduct *is* considered serious enough for a community sentence, an action plan order is likely to be considered as a first option.

Written reports

Before making an action plan order, the court must receive a written report (not necessarily a PSRs as such) prepared by a probation officer, social worker or member of a YOT. This report will outline the proposed requirements of the order, the benefits for the offender and the attitude of the offender's parents or guardians to it. A written report which proposes an action plan order should:

- set out the requirements that might be imposed on the juvenile, including reparation to the victim
- indicate what these requirements are intended to achieve and how they will help secure the young person's rehabilitation or prevent further offending
- comment on the extent to which parents or guardians are likely to support or help the juvenile to comply with the requirements and their willingness to do so; and
- if the offender is under the age of 16, the report should also include information about the offender's family circumstances, and the effect which the proposed requirements of the order might be expected to have on those circumstances.

When specifying the requirements to be included in the order, the court will endeavour to avoid any conflict with the offender's religious beliefs, education or employment times, and the requirements of any other community sentence to which he or she may be subject.

The report writer should also cover the question of reparation to the victim, and where this is proposed should indicate whether the victim does consent. The report writer will also want to consider whether there are any merits in recommending a parenting order (p.102-104). The three months action plan may include requirements that the offender participate in activities specified in the order at a fixed time and place. These might include such things as anger management classes, motor education projects and drug or alcohol misuse programmes. Another specified requirement that may be included is that the offender should present himself or herself, at certain specified times and places to people specified in the order. The object might be to help the offender establish a routine in what may have been a chaotic lifestyle.

Other requirements that may be included are that:

- the offender should attend an attendance centre for a specified number of hours. This cannot be included unless the offence was punishable with imprisonment in the case of an adult.
- the offender should stay away from a specified place or places. This would include such places as shopping centres or amusement arcades.

- the offender should comply with specified educational arrangements. This will cover offenders who have been truanting and committing crime while absent from their educational establishment.
- the offender should make reparation to a specified person or persons, or to the community at large.

The 1998 Act also empowers the court to fix a further hearing, not more than 21 days after the making of the order, where it will consider a report prepared by the responsible officer, and, on his or her application or that of the offender, may then cancel or insert any provisions which appear in the light of that report to be necessary.

Breach
It is a duty of the responsible officer to apply to the court to bring breach proceedings where it is alleged that there is failure to comply with an action plan order. In dealing with breach proceedings a court may:

- whether or not it decides to vary or discharge the order, impose a fine up to a maximum of £1,000 or impose an attendance centre order or a curfew order on the offender
- where the action plan order was made by the youth court, discharge the action plan order and deal with the offender in any way in which it could originally have dealt with him or her if the action plan order had not been made; or
- if the order was made by the Crown Court, commit the offender in custody or release him or her on bail until he or she can be brought before the Crown Court.

Pilot schemes
Action plan orders are being piloted, in specified areas, for 18 months from 30 September 1998 with a view to nationwide implementation in 2000/2001.

Drug Treatment and Testing Orders

The Crime and Disorder Act 1998 introduced this new community penalty which is aimed at those who are convicted of crime/crimes to fund their drug habit and who show a willingness to co-operate with treatment. It is to be phased in: see *Pilot schemes*, below and 📖✍.

The offender must be aged 16 years or over and the order will have effect for between six months and three years.

The court is enabled with the offender's consent, to make an order requiring him or her to undergo treatment for a drug problem either in tandem with another community order (especially probation or supervision), or on its own. Once agreed to, the testing is mandatory.

The court must be satisfied that arrangements for implementing the order have been made in the relevant area.

The offence need not be imprisonable but as it is a 'community order' the offence or offences must pass the 'serious enough' test.

The offender must be dependent on drugs or have a propensity to misuse them and such dependency/propensity must require and be susceptible to treatment. In order to ascertain dependency or propensity the court may, provided the offender is willing, require him or her to provide samples. Whilst not specified in the 1998 Act there must presumably be some actual or assumed nexus between drugs and the individual's offending.

Nature of the order
The drug treatment and testing order must include:

- a *treatment requirement* stating whether this will be residential or non-residential and the identity of the treatment provider;
- a *testing requirement* with a specified frequency of drug testing; and
- a provision specifying the petty sessional area where the offender will reside.

A minimum frequency of the provision of samples each month must be specified. The order must also specify that, for the treatment and testing period, the offender shall be under probation supervision, and the responsible officer must be informed of the result of tests.

Proof of drug misuse is not essential for the court to make the order. The offender will have to consent to the order and the treatment provider's assessment will have to accompany/be incorporated in the PSR in order that the court can be satisfied that the offender is susceptible to treatment and that there is a place on a treatment programme.

The treatment provider will be the main supervisor of testing and will decide when and where the tests, to be randomly allocated, are taken, subject to the court's testing requirement. Treatment providers may take as many tests as they wish, but they must take the minimum number of tests required by the court and submit the results to the supervising probation officer who will report them to the court. In addition, the offender must report to a probation officer as required by him or her and notify the probation officer of any change of address.

The offender is required to attend review hearings which are held at least once a month. At these hearings the court may amend the order. If the offender fails to express willingness to comply with whatever the court proposes by way of amendment, the court may revoke the order and the offender can be re-sentenced. In this eventuality the court should take into account the extent of any compliance with the order. The re-sentence could include a custodial sentence provided the original offence was imprisonable in the case of an adult.

In the event of the court receiving satisfactory reviews, it may decide that subsequent reviews should take place without a formal hearing. It can, at any time in the future, reverse this decision if necessary. Even where there is no hearing, the supervising officer will still make a written report to the court.

Explanation to the offender

A court intending to make a drug treatment and testing order must explain in ordinary language:

- the affect and meaning of its requirements
- the consequences of failure to comply with the order; and
- the powers of the court to review the order.

As well as the offender indicating that he or she is willing to comply with the order, copies must also be given to him or her, the treatment provider and the supervising probation officer.

Pilot schemes

Drug treatment and testing orders are being piloted in specified areas of the country. These pilots will last 18 months from the 30 September 1998, with a view to national implementation from 2000 onwards if the pilot schemes are considered satisfactory when evaluated.

Supervision Orders

A supervision order can be made in relation to an offender aged ten to 17 inclusive. These orders have been a cornerstone of developments in relation to juvenile offenders. They provide a demanding but constructive option, particularly when extra requirements are added to the order. There is no minimum period and the maximum period is three years. The supervisor will be a local authority social worker or a probation officer depending on local arrangements and, in future, arrangements vis-à-vis the local YOT. A supervision order may include requirements for the juvenile:

- to live at a particular place
- to attend at a specified place at specified times
- to take part in various forms of activity (including in some instances highly intensive programmes of supervised activities).

The court may insert such requirements in the order, or it may delegate to the supervisor the discretion to require the juvenile to do any or all of the above things. The maximum number of days on which the juvenile may be required to comply with such directions is 90 (not necessarily consecutive) days.

Attending and participating requirements are sometimes called 'intermediate treatment', or IT: either 'discretionary IT' or 'court stipulated IT'. Requirements for stipulated IT are also known as 'specified activities requirements'.

The court may also require the child or young person:

- to remain at home for specified periods of not more than ten hours between 6pm and 6am for not more than 30 (not necessarily consecutive) days in the first three months
- to refrain from taking part in specified activities, either on a stipulated day or days, or during the whole or a stipulated part of the supervision order (the 90 day limit does not apply to these requirements).

More than one requirement may be attached at the same time. Before including any of the above requirements (other than those at the supervisor's discretion) the court must obtain the offender's consent and consult the supervisor about the offender's circumstances and the feasibility of securing his or her compliance. It must consider the requirements necessary for securing the offender's good conduct or for preventing the juvenile committing further offences. The court may also require the juvenile:

- to receive psychiatric treatment, where the youth court is satisfied on medical evidence that the offender's mental condition requires and is susceptible to treatment. Where the young person is 14 or over, his or her consent is required.
- to attend school or comply with other arrangements made for his or her education, where the offender is of compulsory school age. The consent of the child or young person is not required, but the court must consult the local education authority and the supervisor before imposing such a requirement.

Reparation

The Crime and Disorder Act 1998 has strengthened the supervision order by enabling conditions requiring reparation to the victim of the offence or to the community at large, to be attached as part of the order. These new requirements cover the same ground as reparation orders (see this chapter at p.150) but here they form an integral part of the supervision order and are therefore subject to the 90 day maximum number of days on which such requirements can be imposed. These new reparation conditions will await developments with the piloting of reparation orders for 18 months from the 30 September 1998 with a view to national implementation during 2000/20001: 📖✋ .

Residence requirements

The Children Act 1989 empowered courts to include a 'residence requirement' in supervision orders. This requires the supervised person to live in accommodation provided by or on behalf of the local authority for a specified period not exceeding six months. The court can specify named people with whom the offender may not live. This requirement can be attached to a supervision order provided that:

- the youth court is of the opinion that the offence is serious
- it is satisfied that the offending is due to a significant extent to the circumstances in which the child or young person has been living; and
- when the offender committed the offence, he or she was subject to a supervision order containing a residence requirement or another requirement (other than requirements at the supervisor's discretion, or for mental treatment or school attendance).

Before making a residence requirement the court must consult the local authority and obtain and consider a PSR. This requirement *cannot* be dispensed with: neither will an earlier report suffice: in contrast to the situation in relation to other forms of community orders: see p.68.

The Crime and Disorder Act 1998 contains provisions to strengthen the residence requirements of a supervision order (section 71). It simplifies the conditions which must be satisfied before courts can impose a requirement to live in local authority accommodation as part of a supervision order. It is anticipated that these changes will come into effect on 1 April 1999. From the implementation date a court will be able to impose a requirement to live in local authority accommodation as part of a supervision order where the juvenile has:

- previously been the subject of a supervision order which imposed a requirement, and
- failed to comply with that requirement or is found guilty of an offence committed whilst the supervision order was in force

and in either event the court is satisfied that the failure to comply with the requirement or the offending behaviour was due to a significant extent to the young person's living arrangements and that the residence requirement would assist rehabilitation .

National Standards

A *National Standard for Supervision Orders* has been promulgated under the joint auspices of the Home Office, Department of Health and Welsh Office. This describes the objectives of supervision orders as:

- enabling and encouraging the young offender to understand and accept responsibility for his or her behaviour and its consequences
- ensuring the involvement, wherever possible, of the parents, guardian, family or other carers in the supervision of the young offender
- helping the young offender to resolve personal difficulties linked with offending and to acquire positive new skills
- making the young offender aware of the impact of the crime on its victims, the community and the offender himself or herself
- motivating and assisting the young offender towards a greater sense of personal responsibility, discipline and self-respect, to aid reintegration as a law-abiding member of the community
- ensuring that the young offender understands the difference between right and wrong and that the supervision programme is demanding and effective.

Breaches of requirements of supervision orders

The Crime and Disorder Act 1998 has significantly revised breach proceedings to include a power to discharge the order and to re-sentence. Under section 72 of the 1998 Act, the court may, on breach:

- vary the supervision order
- impose a fine of up to £1,000, a curfew order or an attendance centre order in addition to the supervision order
- discharge the order and re-sentence for the original offence, or where the original order was made by the Crown Court the youth court may commit the offender to the Crown Court to be dealt with.

Probation Orders

A probation order is available where the juvenile is aged 16 or 17. The probation order is a sentence in its own right—and not, as was once the case, an order in lieu of sentence. A probation order can be made whether or not the maximum sentence for the offence includes imprisonment in the case of an adult. The statutory purposes of probation are:

- to secure the offender's rehabilitation; or
- to protect the public from harm from the offender; or

• to prevent further offences by the offender.

Effect of a probation order
The offender is placed under the supervision of a probation officer for the area in which he or she resides or will reside. He or she must keep in touch with the supervising officer in accordance with such instructions as the officer may give, and notify the officer of any change of address—sometimes called 'standard conditions'.

Duration
A probation order lasts for such period as the court decides—not less than six months nor more than three years. A three year order may represent a considerable burden ('restriction of liberty') to a 16 or 17 year old.

Pre-sentence reports and probation orders
Strictly speaking, only probation orders containing additional requirements must by law be preceded by a PSR (subject to the same cautionary rider about dispensing with PSRs in the case of a juvenile which appears under the heading *Pre-sentence reports and suitability* above). Seemingly, most courts accept that it is usually undesirable to make even a basic probation order without full information, and particularly in the case of a juvenile. Care must be taken about what is said when calling for a pre-sentence report: *Chapter 6.*

Additional requirements
If felt desirable for any of the statutory purposes of probation (above) the court may insert one or more additional requirements:

• *a requirement as to residence.* This could be:
—residence in an approved probation hostel managed by the probation service or a voluntary organization.
—at a non approved hostel or other institution such as a dependency clinic which may tackle drug or alcohol addictions (some of which are private organizations)
—a requirement to reside where directed or approved by the probation officer. This is likely to be in the offender's home area at a private address considered suitable by the probation officer and will restrict the offender from moving without first seeking approval from the probation officer.

• *a requirement to attend (i) a probation centre or (ii) other specified activities for up to 60 days*
—a probation centre is a resource approved by the Secretary of State offering an intensive programme which addresses offending

behaviour and its various causes. Offenders are expected to attend for a full day and for as many days as necessary (up to 60 days in all) to complete the programme. Probation centres are generally regarded as being for those at the top end of the 'serious enough' scale.

—specified activities are approved locally by the probation committee. Offenders can be required to attend a specified activity—e.g. an alcohol education group—for up to 60 days or a range of activities according to their needs (e.g. an offending behaviour group, an anger management course, a substance misuse group). A session lasting for, say, two hours counts as a day.

—there is one exception to the 60 day maximum rule and this applies to sex offenders. There is no upper limit on the number of days for which attendance can be required (subject to this not exceeding the length of the probation order), but the court which imposes the requirement must specify the number of days the offender is required to attend a sex offenders' group (or other facility) when making the order.

• *a requirement to receive psychiatric treatment.* This condition can only be used when the court has an assessment from a psychiatrist and treatment is actually available. Again, the requirement can be for the whole length of the probation order or for a part of this time as specified by the court.

• *a requirement to receive treatment for drug or alcohol dependency.* This refers to day or residential facilities—usually for the seriously addicted. There is no restriction on the length of the requirement. It can be for the complete duration of the probation order or for a specific part of it, as determined by the court.

Other requirements
Courts have a general discretion to construct other requirements to meet special needs within the overall purposes of a probation order. This should not be used to circumvent any of the statutory requirements.

Community Service Orders

A community service order is available where the juvenile is aged 16 or 17. Under the order the juvenile is required to perform unpaid work in the community. A probation officer or someone employed by the probation service oversees the order (other day-to-day arrangements may exist as a result of multi-agency arrangements, but the ultimate responsibility falls on the probation service). The juvenile must keep in touch with the relevant officer in accordance with instructions and notify him or her of any change of address. The juvenile must perform the hours of work as instructed, but such instructions must, so far as practicable, not conflict with work, education or the offender's religious beliefs. The order has no inherent welfare content—and is mainly concerned with punishment and reparation.

Duration

The minimum number of hours is 40 and the maximum 240 (it was formerly 120 for 16-year-olds but this was increased in 1992 when the age limit for the youth court was raised so as to include 17 year olds). The work must be performed within 12 months of the order being made, although the order remains in effect until the work is completed. It is possible to impose consecutive periods whether made on the same occasion or previously. Legal advice is desirable: 📖✍.

Imprisonable offences

A community service order can only be made if the maximum sentence for the offence includes imprisonment in the case of an adult. However, these orders are no longer viewed as 'alternatives to custody' (as they once were) but as sentences in their own right.

Pre-sentence reports and 'assessment' for community service

A PSR is required before imposing a community service order unless the court deems such a report to be unnecessary (and subject to the cautionary rider about dispensing with such reports in the case of a juvenile: see *Pre-sentence reports and suitability* above). There is, in any event, with community service a quite separate requirement whereby the court must be satisfied that the offender is a suitable person to perform work under such an order and that work is available—often called a 'community service assessment' (which, unlike the PSR itself, can be oral or written: although often incorporated in the PSR). Care must be taken as to what is said when calling for a pre-sentence report or community service assessment: *Chapter 6*.

Explanations

The youth court must explain the way in which it proposes to deal with the juvenile and allow representations.

Combination Orders

The combination order combines elements of the probation order and the community service order. This is the *only* way in which probation and community service can be imposed together for a single offence. There are no specific statutory purposes for combination orders, but the fact that the order incorporates elements of probation means that the purposes set out in relation to *Probation Orders* (above) are incorporated into the thinking behind that part of the order. There is a single order even though the constituent parts will be supervised and monitored separately. The juvenile is subject to the same obligations for each part of the order as he or she would be if each had been made independently. Thus e.g. restrictions concerning the effect of the community service part of the order on work, education and religion equally apply.

Conditions can be added to the probation part of the order (see *Probation Orders* above)—although attention must be paid to the total restriction on liberty. This is a particularly acute consideration in the case of a juvenile who may experience such a combination in an onerous way.

Community service cannot be combined with a supervision order to a local authority for the same offence. Given the 'lack of maturity' conclusion which is likely to precipitate a supervision order for a 16 or 17 year old, it would seem inconsistent to combine such orders for separate offences dealt with on the same occasion.

Duration
A combination order involves:

- a probation element of *at least* 12 months (as opposed to six months for 'straight' probation) and up to three years.
- a community service element of between 40 and 100 hours (compared to 240 hours maximum re 'simple' community service).

Restriction of liberty and suitability
The nature of the combination order means that care needs to be taken when assessing the extent of restriction on liberty and the suitability of what may be a particularly demanding order for a juvenile—especially if requirements are to be added to the probation part of the order. The outcome must not be wholly *disproportionate* to the offence.

Imprisonable offences
The maximum sentence for the offence must include imprisonment in the case of an adult.

Pre-sentence reports for combination orders
A PSR is required before imposing a combination order unless the court deems such a report to be unnecessary (and subject to the same caution when considering dispensing with such reports in the case of a juvenile mentioned under *Pre-sentence reports and suitability* above).

There is, in any event, a separate requirement whereby the court must be satisfied in respect of the community service element that the offender is a suitable person to perform work under that part of the order and also that work is available—usually on the basis of a community service assessment. This part of the assessment may be oral or written. In practice it may form part of the main PSR.

Willingness to comply
As with most community orders, consents etc. are no longer needed. Given the high level of restriction of liberty involved an indication of the juvenile's/parent's etc. readiness for what lies ahead may be advisable

Curfew Orders

The curfew order provisions are in force but only of practical effect where courts have been notified that monitoring arrangements, electronic or otherwise, are available in individual areas. Trials began in three areas of England and Wales in July 1995. When in force, curfew orders will be available for 16 and 17-year-olds.

Effect of a curfew order
The juvenile is required to remain, for periods specified in the order, at a particular place (usually, but not necessarily, his or her home) or places. Different places may be specified for different periods. The order is monitored by a person selected from a list of people specified for that purpose by the Home Secretary. Such people may be drawn from the private sector.

If the court so orders, monitoring may include electronic 'tagging' of the offender. There are restrictions comparable to those which apply to community service (above) concerning the effect on work, education and religion.

Duration
The order can be for between two and 12 hours a day which may be spread over one or more blocks. It can last for up to six months.

No need for an imprisonable offence
Curfew orders can be made in respect of *any* offence whether or not the maximum sentence includes imprisonment in the case of an adult—although the 'serious enough' test for a community sentence must be satisfied and the court needs to consider, in particular, the extent of restriction of liberty, particularly in relation to a juvenile who may experience the order in an onerous way.

Pre-sentence reports

There is no obligation to obtain a PSR. However, the court must obtain information about the place which it is proposed to specify in the order, and the effect that the order will have on people likely to be affected by the offender's presence at that place—pointing to the desirability of a PSR, especially in the case of a juvenile.

Attendance Centre Orders

The purpose of an attendance centre order is that the offender should be 'given, under supervision, appropriate occupation and instruction'. The order requires attendance at a specified centre and compliance with its rules. These Home Office run centres are normally staffed by the police, sometimes with an input from other agencies. The regime is typically one of discipline, physical training, social awareness and social skills.

A centre must be available to the court (in practice there must be one in the juvenile's home area: not every area has one) and within reasonable travelling distance for the offender: see below. Liaison arrangements serve to provide magistrates with knowledge of local provision and an idea of the regime involved. In future, there is likely to be a solid connection with the local YOT in view of police involvement.

Duration

Attendance centre orders are available for offenders aged ten to 20 years inclusive, but there are separate 'junior attendance centre' facilities for people below the age of 18. In the case of a juvenile, the order must be for 12 hours unless:

- where the offender is aged ten to 13 years the youth court is of the opinion, having regard to age and other circumstances, that 12 hours is excessive. The hours may then be reduced below 12.
- in the case of any juvenile offender the court considers, having regard to all the circumstances, that 12 hours is inadequate. It then has power to increase the order up to 24 hours.
- in the case of a 16 or 17-year-old the court considers, having regard to all the circumstances, that 12 hours (and in practice 24 hours) is inadequate. It then has power to increase the order up to 36 hours (which is also the maximum period for people aged up to 20).

The court must fix the time of the first attendance but the centre organizer determines the length of attendances and further dates. There is a maximum attendance of three hours on any one day.

There is provision for attendance by females in some areas: 📖✍.

Pre-sentence reports and attendance centre orders
A PSR is not a prerequisite but is desirable in the case of a juvenile (compare the cautionary rider about dispensing with such reports in the case of a juvenile under the heading *Pre-sentence reports and suitability* above). Special attention should be paid to the following requirements:

- the centre must be reasonably accessible to the offender having regard to means of access, age and other relevant circumstances (centres for females, or 'mixed centres', are less common than those for males, particularly for juveniles)
- as far as practicable, attendance must not interfere with school or work hours.

Imprisonable offences
The maximum sentence for the offence must include imprisonment in the case of an adult.

BREACH OF COMMUNITY ORDERS

For breach purposes, each community order is a self-contained disposal. Re-offending during the currency of an order does not, in itself, amount to a breach. Different provisions apply to failures re different orders:

Probation, community service, combination and curfew
Failure 'without reasonable excuse' by a juvenile to comply with a requirement of any of these orders can, on the matter being returned to court, result in one of the following outcomes:

- no action
- a fine of up to £1,000 (14 to 17 year olds); £250 in the case of someone below the age of 14
- a community service order for up to 60 hours
- an attendance centre order.

In each case the original community order continues to run. However, the court has the option to revoke the order and to re-sentence for the original offence. There is a requirement to give credit to the extent, if any, to which compliance occurred. Alternatively, where:

- the offence carries imprisonment; and
- failure to comply is found by the court to be 'wilful and persistent'

the court may revoke the original community order and re-sentence, dealing with the offender as if he or she had just refused consent to a community order: a basis for a custodial sentence (provided available for the juvenile in question): see under *Custody*, below—and even if the original offence did not warrant custody. The original offence must carry imprisonment. Credit must be given re any part of the order served.

Attendance centre orders
Failure to attend or comply with the rules of the centre may result in:

- a fine of up to £1,000 (14 to 17 year olds); £250 in the case of someone below the age of 14
- revocation and re-sentencing for the original offence. There are provisions analogous to those for other community orders, above, whereby credit must be given to the extent that compliance has occurred, and allowing a custodial sentence to be imposed if the failure was 'wilful and persistent'.

AMENDMENT ETC. OF COMMUNITY ORDERS

There is provision for amending supervision, probation, community service, combination and curfew orders. The provisions also cover revocation on application by the offender or supervisor if there is a subsequent change in circumstances. Revocation can be ordered on its own, or coupled with re-sentencing depending on the circumstances. In some instances a subsequent court, on sentencing an offender to an immediate custodial sentence, can revoke an earlier order but has no power to re-sentence for the original offence in such circumstances.

Attendance centre orders have their own code for amendment and revocation. Generally speaking: 📖✋.

The arrangements for reviewing or altering the terms of *Action Plan Orders* and *Drug Treatment and Testing Orders* are outlined under each of those headings, above.

Custody 📖✋

THRESHOLD CRITERIA: there are three bases for using custody as follows:

- the offence, or the combination of the offence and one or more offences associated with it, is so serious that *only* such a sentence can be justified (the 'so serious' test); or
- the offence is a sexual or violent offence (both widely defined by the Criminal Justice Act 1991: but seek advice) and only such a sentence would be adequate to protect the public from serious harm from the offender (the 'protection of the public' test); or
- following refusal to consent to a community sentence which requires such consent (or on breach of a community order for an imprisonable offence for 'wilful and persistent' failure to comply with the order).

RESTRICTION ON LIBERTY: the restriction on liberty resulting from custody is obvious—in that the offender is deprived of his or her physical freedom.

SPECIAL CONSIDERATIONS AFFECTING JUVENILES: The basic criteria for custody for both juveniles and adults are the same but there is a different scheme of custodial provision.

The standard provision is *detention in a young offender institution* (YOI). The minimum age is 15. The minimum sentence is two months (so that custody must really be called for) and the maximum six months per offence in the youth court: but see further in the text. A juvenile is normally released after serving half of his or her sentence. All such offenders are subject to supervision following release.

Secure training orders exist for twelve to 14 year olds. Additional criteria apply before they can be used (p.141).

When *detention and training orders* are introduced (p.142), secure training orders and detention in a young offender institution will be abolished

There is no power to suspend the operation of custodial sentence on a juvenile.

Associated offences

This term has the meaning outlined at p.95.

DETENTION IN A YOI

Offenders under 18 can be sentenced to periods of detention in a young offender institution of up to six months. This increases to 12 months in aggregate where there are two or more indictable only or either way offences for which the youth court is sentencing on the same occasion.

The minimum sentence is two months. This is designed to prevent very short sentences for juveniles and to force courts only to use the facility when the seriousness of the offence or the protection of the public truly warrants more than a nominal sentence.

The minimum age for detention in a young offender institution is 15 years and the provision is available for either sex.

The Crown Court can sentence a juvenile to up to two years detention for a single offence. The youth court has power to commit a juvenile to the Crown Court for sentence: see later in this chapter.

The Crown Court also has power to sentence to long-term detention for certain *Grave Crimes,* see *Chapter 5,* p.55.

Imprisonable offences
The offence must be imprisonable in the case of an adult. The statute creating the offence will state whether it attracts imprisonment.

Procedural requirements
Before imposing custody, the youth court must take into account all information available to it regarding the circumstances of the *offence* or *offences,* including aggravating or mitigating factors. It may take into account any mitigating factors concerning the *offender.* It may also take into account any information before it about the *offender* where, in the case of a sexual or violent offence, custody or longer custody is being considered to protect the public from serious harm from him or her.

'Sexual offence' and 'violent offence'—definitions
The Criminal Justice Act 1991 lists those sexual offences to which the protection of the public ground applies (the list covers most sexual offences—but not e.g. indecent exposure). Violent offences are widely defined to cover situations where an offence 'leads, or is intended or likely to lead' to death or physical injury (including arson). Protection from 'serious harm' means from 'death or serious injury, whether physical or psychological'. Court legal advisers will normally anticipate situations where definition is likely to be a live issue: 📖✍.

Legal representation
There is a *always* a restriction on imposing custody on a juvenile where he or she is not legally represented after a finding of guilt. (This contrasts

with the position in relation to adults where the requirement applies only to a first custodial sentence).

In the unlikely event that the juvenile is not already represented by the time the youth court reaches the conclusion that custody is a possibility, the court should explain the effect of this provision—with a warning to use the opportunity which the court is obliged to give by way of adjournment to acquire representation (if need be by applying for legal aid). Failure to obtain representation, to apply for legal aid, or refusal of legal aid on grounds of means will allow a subsequent court, if it considers it appropriate, to impose custody without the juvenile being represented. The juvenile can waive these rights by declaring an unwillingness to consult a solicitor or to apply for legal aid—although it may be sensible to encourage the offender to consult the duty solicitor or probation officer before proceeding.

Pre-sentence reports (PSRs)

The court must obtain a PSR before deciding that either of the first two criteria for custody above (i.e. the 'so serious' or 'protection of the public' test) is made out—unless it deems a PSR to be unnecessary. The youth court can only do this if an earlier report (or the latest in a series of earlier reports) is available, which it then considers. Juveniles' lives can change rapidly, and good practice indicates that a report should be obtained wherever possible. Failure to comply with the PSR requirements does not, of itself, render the order invalid but a fresh report will need to be obtained if there is an appeal. For further details, see *Chapter 6, Procedures, Information and Evidence.*

The report is similarly needed in order to assess the appropriate *length* of the custodial sentence.

There is no comparable legal requirement for a PSR before deciding on a custodial sentence for failure to consent to a community sentence, or for wilful and persistent failure to comply with such a sentence, although there will need to be evidence of the failure and other relevant circumstances. Again, in the case of a juvenile a PSR is always desirable.

Care must be taken as to what is said when calling for a PSR. In particular, if a custodial sentence is considered an option at this stage, nothing should be said which gives the juvenile the expectation of a non-custodial sentence. The safest course is to expressly preserve all options, while considering whether a *provisional* indication of seriousness can be given to assist the PSR writer: see also the discussion at pp.68-74.

Length of custodial sentences

Custodial sentences take effect straight away (and, where there are two or more such sentences, *concurrently* to one another unless the court has specifically ordered that they take effect *consecutively:* below).

The seriousness of the offence or, as appropriate, the need to protect the public from serious harm from the perpetrator of a sexual or violent offence should determine the length of any custodial sentence within the maximum sentence available. The protection of the public criterion allows a sentence longer than would be justified by the seriousness of the offence in respect of a sexual or violent offence.

Orders for detention in a young offender institution which are possible in the youth court are as follows:

- detention may be imposed for any period from a minimum of two months to the maximum available on summary conviction (this is usually fixed by statute at from one month to six months per offence)
- periods can be ordered to take effect consecutively to:
  —previous sentences (i.e. those imposed on an earlier occasion: when there is no overall aggregate limit)
  —other sentences passed on the same occasion subject to the following limits:
  (a) six months in aggregate; or
  (b) normally 12 months in aggregate where there are two or more indictable offences: 📖🖐 .

The length of other custodial sentences, i.e. secure training orders and detention and training orders are discussed later in this section.

Concurrent and consecutive sentences

As indicated, the youth court can order periods of detention in a young offender institution to be served concurrently to one another or consecutively (i.e. within the youth court's maximum powers: above). The decision is a judicial one, and in the latter case, it must be clearly stated that the sentences are consecutive. In practice, sentences are usually ordered to take effect concurrently unless there is a specific reason for them to be made consecutive. This will primarily depend on the court's assessment of the combined seriousness of the particular offences under consideration, or, as the case may be in sexual or violent cases, the extent to which there is a need to protect the public from serious harm from the offender.

See later in this section for concurrent and consecutive sentences of secure training and detention and training.

Short local detention

There is no power to place juveniles in short local detention (as there is in the case of adults). However, older juveniles may become adults by the time fine default proceedings occur when local detention is possible: see under *Fines, General enforcement powers* earlier in this section.

Custody and mentally disordered offenders

Where the offender is or appears to be mentally disordered the court is obliged *in addition to the standard procedures for custody* to:

- obtain and consider a medical report from a registered medical practitioner approved for the purposes of the Mental Health Act 1983 unless it considers such a report to be unnecessary
- consider, in any event, all information before it relating to the offender's mental condition; and
- consider what treatment may be available.

Mental disorder is a specialist area invariably requiring advice: 📖✍.

Explanations and reasons for decisions

The youth court must explain the way in which it intends to deal with the juvenile and allow representations: *Chapter 6, Procedures, Information and Evidence*. In addition, whenever it passes a custodial sentence it is required to state in open court:

- that it is of opinion that either or both of the 'so serious' or 'protection of the public' grounds for custody apply; and
- why it is of that opinion.

It must also explain to the offender in ordinary language why it is passing a custodial sentence. The reasons are specified in the relevant warrant and entered in the court register. There is a duty to give extra reasons where the court passes a sentence for a sexual or violent offence which is longer than is commensurate with the seriousness of the offence. Again, this must also be explained in ordinary language.

Clearly, all such reasons and explanations must be valid in the sense that they are properly relevant and supportable in law. The youth court should thus, as a matter of good practice, check their intentions with the court legal adviser: 📖✍.

Failure to comply with post release supervision

There is automatic supervision of juvenile offenders on release from detention. This supervision is by a probation officer, local authority social worker or member of a YOT.

Where the offender is not released under any form of licence, the period of supervision is normally three months. If the offender is released under licence, the normal rules governing this apply instead. However, if the licence period is for less than three months, a period of supervision will commence when the licence ends and terminate three months after release.

In the event of a failure to comply with the requirements of supervision an offence is deemed to be committed with the maximum penalty of up £1,000 (i.e. young persons) (January, 1999) or 30 days custody. No other penalties can be imposed. Special provisions relate to *Secure Training Orders* and *Detention and Training Orders:* see under those headings.

SECURE TRAINING ORDERS

This sentence for persistent young offenders was introduced by the Criminal Justice and Public Order Act 1994. When detention and training orders (see next section) come into force, they will replace both secure training orders and detention in a young offender institution for offenders under the age of 18.

Criteria for a secure training order

The main features of secure training orders are as follows:

- the offence must be an imprisonable offence in the case of an adult
- it must be so serious that only a custodial sentence is appropriate.
- it must have been committed on or after 1 March 1998
- the offender must be aged 12 but under 15 at the time of conviction
- the offender must have been not less than 12 at the time of committing the offence
- the offender must be convicted of three or more offences which are imprisonable in the case of an adult
- either on this or a previous occasion, the offender must have been:
  (a) found by the court to be in breach of a supervision order under the CYPA 1969; or
  (b) convicted of an imprisonable offence whilst on supervision.

Minimum and maximum length of secure training orders

The minimum sentence length is six months, and the maximum is two years. The first half of the order is served in detention at a secure training centre.[2] The second half of the order involves compulsory supervision in the community. Before an order can be imposed, there must be suitable accommodation available, either in a secure training centre or in local authority secure accommodation. The court is required to check the availability of places in both with the Juvenile Offenders Unit of the Home Office, before passing sentence. It follows that if the secure training centre is full, the court can commit the offender to a local authority secure unit until a place becomes available.

---

[2] At the time of writing only one secure training centre exists, at Cookham Wood in Kent.

Breach of supervision aspect

Breach of the supervision requirements in the second part of the order enables a youth court to:

(a) order the offender to be detained for a further period not exceeding the shorter of three months or the remainder of the period of secure training order as the court may specify; or

(b) impose a Level 3 fine.

DETENTION AND TRAINING ORDERS

The detention and training order (not yet in force) was introduced by sections 73 to 79 Crime and Disorder Act 1998. It provides for a single new custodial sentence for ten to 17 year olds which will replace the existing sentences of secure training and detention in a young offender institution for people under the age of 18.

A detention and training order can be made in respect of:

- *15 to 17-year-olds* for any imprisonable offence which is so serious as to justify a custodial sentence
- *12 to 14-year-olds* who, in the opinion of the court, are persistent offenders for offences so serious as to justify a custodial sentence
- *10 and 11-year-olds* for persistent offenders, but only when the court considers that custody is the only method of protecting the public from further offending.

The Home Secretary will determine whether this section ever needs to be introduced in relation to ten and eleven year olds.

Both the youth court and Crown Court can impose detention and training orders.

Length of detention and training orders

The length of the sentence imposed is determined by the 1998 Act, and can be for periods of four, six, eight, ten, 12, 18 and 24 months only. The sentence must not exceed the maximum term fixed by statute in the case of an adult.

These specified periods of detention are not without difficulty. The kind of problems envisaged include:

- dealing with a number of offenders and attempting to achieve proper differentials between them, to reflect differences in culpability or mitigation
- making appropriate allowance for a timely guilty plea (p.95)

- consecutive and concurrent sentences: if a defendant is found guilty of more than one offence, or convicted of offences whilst subject to an existing detention and training order, the court has the same power to pass consecutive detention and training orders as if they were sentences of imprisonment, provided the aggregate of two years is not exceeded.

It is clear that a youth court is intended to have power to impose detention and training orders up to the maximum possible term of 24 months, but the power to pass consecutive orders is said to be subject to adult court restrictions in relation to sentences of imprisonment. These, of course, allow a maximum aggregate of 12 months where more than one either way offence is committed.

It could be argued that a youth court could impose concurrent detention and training orders of 24 months each, but consecutive orders may be restricted to 12 months. In the absence of an amendment or different interpretation, this is likely to be tested in the higher courts at an early stage.

When deciding the length of a sentence, courts must take into account time spent on remand, as opposed to the present arrangements, whereby remand time is deducted after a sentence has been imposed.

The Home Secretary will decide where the period of detention and training is to be served, i.e. whether in a secure training centre, a young offender institution, local authority secure accommodation, a youth treatment centre, or any other form of secure accommodation.

Release from detention and training
An offender may be released early or late from such detention on the basis of good progress or otherwise, which will have been set out in a plan or contract at the beginning of the order. The Home Secretary can release offenders one month early for orders of eight months or more but less than 18 months, or either one or two months early for orders of 18 months or longer. He may also apply to the youth court for late release for periods of the same lengths.

Upon release, the young offender is subject to supervision until the end of the order, unless the Home Secretary determines differently. The supervision will be undertaken by either a probation officer, social worker or a member of the local YOT. The offender will be issued with notice of the requirements of supervision, stating who the supervisor is.

Breach of supervision
Breach of supervision after release from custody will give rise to magistrates considering the issue of a summons or warrant to bring the juvenile before the youth court. The penalty for breach is:

- a further period of custody for up to three months, or until the end of the order whichever is the shorter; or
- a Level 3 fine.

Further offences

If an offender is found guilty of a further imprisonable offence during the order, the court can impose an additional period of detention. The maximum length of this detention is equivalent to the length of time between the date of the offence and the end of the order. This period is to be disregarded in sentencing the offender for the new offence, but can be served concurrently or consecutively with any new sentence.

Implementation

These provisions are expected to be implemented for 12-17 year olds in the Summer of 1999. As mentioned earlier, the order will only become available for 10 and 11 year olds if it proves necessary, and by order of the Home Secretary.

COMMITTAL FOR SENTENCE

It will be recalled from *Chapter 5* that there is a special mode of trial procedure in the youth court which applies only to *Grave Crimes* pursuant to section 53 CYPA 1933. This must be understood as an entirely separate code relating only to such matters. There are no general mode of trial provisions in the youth court in relation to either way offences, as there are in the case of an adult in the magistrates' court. However, the youth court does have power to commit a juvenile to the Crown Court for sentence notwithstanding that, initially (and section 53 cases apart) it could not commit to the Crown Court for trial.

The youth court can commit for sentence if it considers that its powers of punishment are insufficient, i.e. in the case of a juvenile aged 15 to 17 years inclusive that more than six months detention is warranted for a single offence, or 12 months in aggregate where two or more either way or indictable only offences are involved. The Crown Court can impose a maximum of two years in a YOI per offence.

Cautionary notes

There may be relatively few cases in practice where the circumstances justify committal to the Crown Court with a view to custody being imposed for between 12 months and two years. It should be specifically noted that the power to commit to the Crown Court for sentence:

- should not be seen by the youth court as a 'get out'

- can only be used where the youth court considers that the offence is so serious that greater punishment should be inflicted than it has power to impose
- does not apply so as to enable committal to the Crown Court for a *longer* sentence to be imposed under the protection of the public limb than is commensurate with the seriousness of the offence (in contrast to the position in relation to adults): seek advice 📖 ⚘
- cannot be used to achieve long term detention, i.e. beyond two years. It is thus extremely important that the court reaches the correct mode of trial decision at the outset in cases where the power to decline jurisdiction under s53 CYPA 1933 and commmit under the grave crimes provisions exists.

Bail or custody
Juveniles can be committed for sentence on bail or in custody: *Chapter 7*.

Abolition of power to commit to the Crown Court for sentence
The power to commit for sentence described in this section will be repealed when schedule 10 to the Crime and Disorder Act 1998 is brought into force. At the time of writing, this has not yet occurred.

VI: COMPENSATION AND REPARATION

Compensation Orders

Payment of compensation by an offender to a victim is a prime consideration in all cases in both the adult court and the youth court when personal injury, loss or damage has resulted from the offence. In the youth court this is subject to additional factors such as the welfare principle and parental responsibility: see *Sections II* and *III* of this chapter. Whatever these considerations, magistrates should always give a high level of attention to this aspect of a case. It can be a salutary lesson if a juvenile has to make recompense to someone who has lost out because of his or her offence—and can in some instances prove to be a constructive approach for all concerned. Compensation can now also be viewed as part of the bigger picture concerning youth justice, in the light of the work of YOTs, police reprimand and warning schemes, reparation orders (see below) and other mechanisms designed to emphasise responsibility to victims and to bring home to offenders the consequences of their behaviour. In practice, magistrates are required and encouraged to award compensation whenever possible. Two factors are particularly important:

- sensitivity to the interest of victims; and

- the financial circumstances of the juvenile (and/or his or her parents or guardians).

The same criteria apply in the youth court as in the adult court, with certain refinements. The court may order a juvenile to pay compensation

> for any personal injury, loss or damage resulting from that offence or any other offence which is taken into consideration by the court determining sentence or to make payments for funeral expenses or bereavement in respect of a death resulting from any such offence, other than a death due to an accident arising out of the presence of a motor vehicle on a road.

The following main points should be noted:

- compensation can be a punishment in its own right or can be ordered to be paid in addition to any other type of sentence. When coupled with some other sentence it is an 'ancillary order'.
- compensation *must* be given preference out of available resources when the court is considering imposing a financial penalty. This means that where both a fine and compensation *are* appropriate, but the juvenile's financial circumstances (or those of the parents or guardians as appropriate) are not sufficient to pay both in full, courts must give priority to a compensation order. It would be wrong to reduce the amount of compensation on grounds of means and to impose a fine as well.
- courts must give reasons for *not* awarding compensation where an award might have been made. These reasons must be announced in court and be recorded in the court register.
- as indictaed in *Section III* of this chapter, parents or guardians are liable to pay compensation in the same circumstances as fines and according to their own financial circumstances as opposed to those of the juvenile. Thus, where a compensation order is made against an offender who is under 16, the court *must* order the parent or guardian to pay the compensation unless it would be unreasonable to do so in the circumstances or the parent or guardian cannot be found. Where the offender is aged 16 or 17 the court *may* order the parent or guardian to pay the compensation.
- in certain circumstances, local authorities with parental responsibility for offenders in their care or accommodation, may be ordered to pay compensation. If so, means are irrelevant. A local authority does not automatically have parental responsibility for a juvenile remanded by a court to their accommodation. Legal advice should be sought if compensation is under consideration in these circumstances: 📖✋.

Maximum amount

The maximum amount of compensation is the same as in the adult court, i.e. £5,000 per offence in respect of which the juvenile has pleaded guilty or been found guilty by the court (January 1999). The total is limited to the maximum that the youth court could order for those offences. However, in setting the amount it may take account of loss stemming from any offences which are being taken into consideration (TICs).

Meaning of personal injury

'Personal injury' includes physical injury and mental injury. An award can be made for terror or distress caused by an offence: 📖✍.

Application

There is no need for a specific application to court (although the prosecutor may often make one on the victim's behalf). The court always has power—of its own motion—to make an award, provided that there is sufficient information to enable it to set a figure. If better evidence of loss, damage or injury, is required it may be appropriate to ask the prosecutor to obtain this (subject to the victim's wishes, if known).

Straightforward cases

Youth courts should order compensation in straightforward cases where the amount can readily be assessed. The power to award compensation represents—in cases where the juvenile's financial circumstances (or those of his or her parents or guardians) are sufficient to meet the award—a speedy means of recompense and avoids the prospect of a separate civil claim by the victim in the county court or High Court.

Road accidents

In most cases compensation arising from road traffic accidents cannot be ordered by magistrates. However, an order can be made in respect of injury, loss or damage (other than that suffered by dependants as a result of death) due to an accident arising out of the presence of a motor vehicle on a road if it is in respect of:

- damage resulting from an offence under the Theft Act 1968 such as the unlawful taking of a motor vehicle (i.e. compensation may relate to the taken vehicle not damage caused by it); or
- injury, loss or damage where
  — the offender is uninsured in relation to the vehicle; and
  — compensation is not payable under the Motor Insurers Bureau Agreement (MIBA). This means that, in respect of property damage, the court is restricted to the first £175 of loss not covered by the MIBA (January, 1999). But this may include any reduction in preferential rates, i.e. loss of 'no claims bonus'.

Fixing the amount

Usually the prosecutor and the juvenile/defence will try to agree the value of any loss. Where there *is* a dispute, the youth court will normally hear evidence presented by the prosecutor. The juvenile may then make representations and/or call evidence. The matter need not be proved to the same standard as the offence in a criminal trial (i.e. beyond reasonable doubt), but there must be some factual basis on which the youth court can arrive at a figure.

When considering a compensation order, the youth court must satisfy itself that actual loss, damage or injury has resulted from the offence. It will look at the cost of replacement or repair of goods damaged. Where items are of sentimental value it may be possible to draw common sense comparisons with other property losses and the likely effect on the victim.

A court can consider lost earnings due to an attack. It can also look at more intangible matters, such as pain and suffering. For further guidance see Home Office Circular 53/1993, the *Magistrates' Association Sentencing Guidelines* and *Guidelines for the Assessment of General Damages in Personal Injury Cases* (Judicial Studies Board: civil cases).

Financial circumstances

The youth court's next obligation is to consider the financial circumstances of the juvenile and of any parent or guardian against whom it is proposed to order compensation. It must have regard to the relevant person's financial circumstances in so far as they appear or are known to the court. The general principles are the same as in relation to *Fines:* see under that heading above. Thus there *may* be a marginally better case for making a *compensation* order which—by way of exception to the normal '12 months rule'—is payable over a longer period, particularly if a parent or guardian has appreciable potential earnings/resources. It cannot be over-stressed that effective use of compensation stems from identifying financial resources which would enable the payer to meet an award. He or she can be required to complete a form setting out their financial circumstances. The court should order payment in part where payment of the whole amount is not a realistic possibility.

Enforcement

Broadly speaking, compensation is enforced in the same way as a fine: pp.111-113. The main differences concern the way such orders can be reviewed (see below). This special procedure apart, compensation cannot be remitted in the ordinary sense: 📖✍.

Compensation ancillary to a custodial sentence

The Court of Appeal has indicated that it is wrong to make a compensation order which will be a burden on release from custody, as this may lead to further offences. It is also not generally appropriate to combine compensation with a substantial sentence in a young offender institution unless immediate funds are also available. If the sentence is short then there may, in a suitable case, be nothing wrong in the youth court fixing an amount which would not be burdensome on release. However, in the case of a juvenile, this needs to be understood in the light of the fact that a parent in the community may be ordered to pay, even whilst the juvenile is in custody.

Appeal

For a note on appeals and their effect on compensation see *Chapter 6*.

Review of compensation orders

The youth court can review a compensation order at the request of the payer, e.g. where a civil court has decided that the injury, loss or damage was less than the value originally placed on it by the youth court; where property has later been recovered, or the means of the payer have deteriorated (seek legal advice if necessary).

Local authorities and compensation

If the local authority has parental responsibility for a juvenile in its care or for whom it has provided accommodation then the court can make a compensation order against the authority unless the court is satisfied that it would be unreasonable to do so having regard to the circumstances of the case. The financial circumstances of the authority are irrelevant.

In 1995, the County Councils in Shropshire and in Lancashire brought a series of appeals in which the High Court quashed compensation orders made against those authorities following findings of guilt recorded against juveniles in their care. The High Court held that where an authority was found to have done everything that it reasonably and properly could to protect the public from the relevant juvenile, it would be unreasonable and unjust that it should be ordered to pay compensation. The High Court also indicated that a local authority's position with regard to young persons in its care was different from that of a natural parent or guardian. A local authority might often be entrusted with the care of, or be obliged to provide accommodation for, a young person who was already an offender or who was of a criminal or anti-social propensity. The steps that the local authority should or could lawfully take to restrain such a young person might well be limited.

It had been submitted that a factor tending towards the imposition of liability upon a local authority to pay compensation was the fact that compensation was designed to compensate the victim. The High Court held that whilst that might be a factor tempting courts to make orders, it was not the correct approach.

A further appeal to the High Court was brought in 1995 by Bedfordshire County Council when it was held that a court should only make a compensation award against a local authority when there was evidence to show that the failure to control the juvenile was a cause of the offending. A court should normally find a causative link between fault and the offending before making a compensation order. If there was no causative fault then it would be unreasonable to make an order.

If the youth court is considering the possibility of a compensation order against a local authority opportunity must be given to the authority to be legally represented so that its views can be clearly expressed. This will usually involve an adjournment. Given the above rulings, youth courts should always seek legal advice: 📖✋.

Reparation Orders

New arrangements for young offenders to make reparation to victims or to the community at large were introduced by sections 67 and 68 Crime and Disorder Act 1998. The purpose of a reparation order is said to be to help young offenders to understand and face up to the consequences of their actions and, in appropriate cases, to offer some practical recompense to victims.

The youth court can make an order requiring an offender to make reparation which is commensurate with the seriousness of the offence(s) for which the order is made. The requirement may not exceed a total of 24 hours in aggregate. Reparation must be made within three months of the order, and requires the consent of the person to whom reparation is to be made.

Suggested examples of reparation include the writing of a letter of apology, a personal apology, or repairing damage. Instead of reparation to the victim, some appropriate activity to the benefit of the community at large may be directed.

A reparation order cannot be combined with a custodial sentence or with a community service order, a combination order, an action plan order or a supervision order with certain requirements (e.g. to live in local authority accommodation, to receive mental treatment, or an education requirement): seek further advice: 📖✋.

Before making a reparation order the Court is required to consider a written report by a probation officer, social worker or member of a YOT. This is designed to cover issues such as the victim's attitude to a possible order. On making the order, the court must explain clearly to the offender the effect of the order, its requirements, how it may be varied and the breach provisions.

The order can be appealed to the Crown Court in the usual way.

Breach of a reparation order
Breach of an order may result in the imposition of a fine not exceeding £1,000 (subject also to age: see p.105), an attendance centre order, a curfew order, or the youth court may discharge the order and deal with the offender afresh for the original offence.

Pilot areas
Reparation orders are being piloted in specified areas of the country for 18 months from the 30 September 1998. National implementation is not expected until the year 2000 at the earliest.

VII: OTHER ORDERS OF THE YOUTH COURT

Binding Over

A juvenile can be bound over to be of good behaviour and to keep the peace in a similar way to an adult. The power can be used on its own (i.e. following a complaint/application by an individual), or, where there is some reason to fear a further breach of the peace, as an adjunct to some other court disposal. Binding over is a form of 'preventive justice'. The person who is bound over promises to keep the peace on pain of forfeiting a sum of money fixed by the court—known as entering into a 'recognisance'. It thus requires the consent of the person whom the court proposes to bind over. In the case of an adult, imprisonment is a sanction in the event of a refusal to be bound over. There is no equivalent sanction in respect of a juvenile. Accordingly, the youth court can only bind over a juvenile if he or she consents to this.

Breach of binding over order
In the event of a breach, the court can order the amount of the recognisance to be forfeited (or 'estreated') in whole or in part.

Legal difficulties
Quite apart from the problems which can arise from the lack of a sanction where a juvenile refuses to be bound over, other problems exist concerning whether the youth court (as opposed to the adult court) has jurisdiction to bind over juveniles or to deal with the breach of a bind over, legal opinion being divided. Such issues will not be settled until there is a ruling from the High Court or legislative provision. Further

technical problems arise e.g. concerning who should conduct binding over proceedings (the Crown Prosecution Service being reluctant to do so in some instances), or who are the parties to any appeal where the court has acted of its own motion. These are compounded by the fact that courts generally have power, in appropriate circumstances, to bind over anyone who is present in court (such as a witness). Further procedural or jurisdictional problems may thus arise where it is a parent or guardian whom it is proposed to bind over. In all cases, magistrates should take legal advice: 📖✋.

Binding over parents to prevent offences

The above powers should not be confused with the specific statutory powers, where an offender is under 18 years of age, to order a parent or guardian to enter into a recognisance to take proper care of or exercise proper control over the juvenile: see *Section III* of this chapter, *Parental Responsibility*.

Binding over parents to ensure compliance with certain orders

Powers to require a parent or guardian to enter into a recognisance to ensure compliance by their child with a community order or to ensure payment of a fine are dealt with earlier in *Section III, Parental Responsibility* and in this section under *Fines*.

Deprivation and Forfeiture Orders

When an offence consists of unlawful possession of property, the court may order the defendant to be deprived of that property. A deprivation order can also be made where property has been used to commit an offence or was intended to be so used, whether or not the defendant has been separately convicted of that other offence.

The court must be satisfied that the property has been lawfully seized from the offender, or was in his or her possession or control when apprehended, or when a summons was issued. An order can also be made in respect of offences taken into consideration (TICs). Common examples include tools used in burglaries or ignition keys used in offences related to the theft or unlawful taking of motor vehicles. There are a number of extra considerations: seek legal advice: 📖✋.

Restitution Orders

Where goods have been stolen and someone is convicted of an offence relating to the theft, the court may order restoration of the goods to the person entitled to them (or of goods bought with any proceeds).

Restitution can also be ordered on conviction for dishonest handling, obtaining by deception or blackmail. There are a number of extra considerations: 📖✋.

Costs

Youth courts have power to award costs, subject to each case being dealt with on its merits. The basic rule is that costs can—and normally should be—awarded in favour of the successful party, including the Crown Prosecution Service (CPS). Costs must always be a reimbursement; i.e. they must not be used as a guise for punishment. Private prosecutors may receive an order that their costs be paid out of central funds (i.e. public monies held by the justices' clerk), but not the CPS or other public authority—they are already funded from the public purse.

Costs against juvenile offenders
The court can order a juvenile to pay just and reasonable costs to the prosecutor. The amount must be stated in the order. If the juvenile is ordered to pay (rather than his or her parent or guardian) then the amount of costs cannot exceed the fine. An order should only be made when the court is satisfied that the offender (or his parent or guardian) has the means to pay. The amount must be stated in the order. Costs cannot be ordered if the offender has been ordered to pay a sum not exceeding £5 (whether by way of fine or compensation) unless the court, in the particular circumstances, considers it right to do so.

The principles covering time for payment of costs are similar to those affecting *Fines:* p.110). It is wrong to order payment if the person required to pay will be unable to do so within a reasonable time (usually in practice within 12 months in the case of adults: so the scope may be less if the juvenile as opposed to a parent or guardian is required to pay).

Defendant's costs orders
Where a case is dismissed, discontinued or withdrawn the court will normally make a 'defendant's costs order' when requested to do so (sometimes called a DCO)—i.e. for payment of his or her costs from central funds (public funds). Only exceptionally will a prosecutor be ordered to pay the defendant's costs instead, e.g. where the prosecutor was negligent in failing to deal with some aspect of the case which would have disclosed a sound defence at an early stage: 📖✋.

Where the juvenile is legally aided
Legal opinion differs on whether and to what extent a juvenile on legal aid should receive a defendant's costs order for items not covered by his or her legal aid order (e.g. pre-legal aid costs, travel to court): 📖✋.

Reasons for not making a DCO

A defendant's costs order is normally made following an acquittal unless there are positive reasons for not doing so, e.g. where the defendant's own conduct has attracted suspicion and misled the prosecutor into thinking that there was a strong case, or the defendant was acquitted on a technicality. Where someone is acquitted on some charges but convicted on others, the court has a discretion whether to make a defendant's costs order or it might order only part of the defendant's costs. In this instance the amount must be specified by the court.

'Taxing' the amount

Unless the order is for an agreed or a part amount, the amount will be determined ('taxed') by the justices' clerk after the defence has submitted a detailed account.

Orders Relating to Mental Disorder 📖🖐

Nowadays, attempts are always made to divert people away from the criminal courts if they are suffering from mental disorder and this applies very strongly in the case of juveniles where the possibility of obtaining a care order in civil proceedings exists in addition to the standard mental health provisions. Many magistrates' courts and youth courts are involved in local liaison, leading e.g. to duty psychiatrist schemes to ensure that medical personnel are in attendance or on call. These arrangements stem from Home Office Circular 66/1990, 'Provision for Mentally Disordered Offenders'. The Crown Prosecution Service also endorses the spirit and objectives of that circular in its own *Code of Practice.*

Ordinary disposals

If a mentally disordered person is capable of being dealt with by the court and is found guilty, all normal disposals apply, including a probation order with a condition of medical or psychiatric treatment. Mentally disturbed offenders cannot be committed to detention simply because of their mental condition—ordinary principles apply as with every other defendant. However, if a court is considering custody, the law obliges it to obtain a psychiatric report.

Special provisions

In addition to its standard sentencing powers, a youth court has power to make the following orders:

- a hospital order whereby the juvenile is detained for medical treatment until discharged by a doctor

- a guardianship order whereby the juvenile is placed under the guardianship of a social services department or an approved person.

A general need for advice 📖✋

If the youth court is considering exercising any of these special powers, it should normally seek legal advice. This advice could cover not only how to obtain the necessary medical reports but all available options such as interim hospital orders and orders of the Crown Court restricting discharge. It should be recognised that many of these problems, particularly in the case of a juvenile, may be resolved by social services departments without the need for court proceedings or via provisions in other disposals such as probation orders and supervision orders with appropriate requirements attached to them.

Deferment of sentence

This option—sparingly used in the adult court—is also available to the youth court. It postpones the whole sentencing process once for up to six months with the consent of the defendant. There is no power of remand and there should be a specific object in mind which should be communicated to the juvenile. Both the welfare principle and the different perception of time to many juveniles suggest that this option should be used even more sparingly, or for a shorter period, in the youth court. If it *is* used and the offender commits another offence during the period of deferment, the court recording the new finding of guilt may deal with the deferred sentence even if the period of deferment has not yet expired.

Anti-Social Behaviour Orders

This new *civil* order introduced by section 1 Crime and Disorder Act 1998, is underpinned by criminal sanctions for breach. The relevant provisions are being implemented on 1 April 1999.

Application is made by the police or local authority in consultation with each other for an order against an individual or a group, such as a family, whose behaviour is anti-social in that, e.g. it has caused alarm, distress or harassment to one or more other people. Whilst it is anticipated that the main use of this remedy will be in respect of adults, it can apply to any person aged ten or over

A statutory defence to an application for an order is available, i.e. that the behaviour was reasonable in the particular circumstances.

Section 4 of the 1998 Act provides for an appeal to the Crown Court.

Part of the court's civil jurisdiction

Application is made by complaint and magistrates will be acting under their *civil* jurisdiction. Where an application is proved, an anti-social behaviour order *may* be made, prohibiting the defendant from doing anything described in the order. The order can last for a specified period of not less than two years, or until further order.

Variation and discharge

application may be made for variation or discharge. Without the consent of both parties an anti-social behaviour order cannot be discharged before the end of the minimum two year period.

Breach of the order

Breach of an anti-social behaviour order renders an adult on summary conviction liable to imprisonment for a term not exceeding six months, or to a fine not exceeding the statutory maximum, or to both. On indictment the maximum imprisonment is five years or a fine or both. It follows that the full range of penalties in the youth court is available for juveniles, subject to the offender's age.

Sex Offender Orders

This new form of order which came into force in December 1998 was created by section 2 Crime and Disorder Act 1998 (with supplemental provisions in section 3). It is unlikely to apply to juveniles, but nothing prevents it from doing so. The police can apply for an order against any sex offender whose present behaviour in the community gives them reasonable cause for concern where they consider that an order is needed to protect the public from serious harm. Again, magistrates will be acting under their *civil* jurisdiction. The order requires the offender to register under the Sex Offenders Act 1997 whilst the order is in effect. The minimum duration for the order is five years. Appeal lies to the Crown Court.

Breach of the order

Breach of such an order without reasonable excuse results in the commission of a criminal offence which, in the case of an adult, is triable either way with a maximum penalty on summary conviction of imprisonment for a term not exceeding six months, or a fine not exceeding the statutory maximum or both. On conviction on indictment, the maximum term of imprisonment is five years and a fine can be imposed instead of or in addition to imprisonment. It follows that the full range of penalties in the youth court will be available for juveniles, subject to the offender's age.

VII: ROAD TRAFFIC CASES:A NOTE

In addition to any penalty, certain motoring offences attract endorsement of the juvenile's driving licence or disqualification. The principles and legal provisions are the same as in the adult court and are not set out here due to their specialist nature.[3] However, a number of points can be noted which are likely to be of special reference to juveniles and of a recurring nature:

- Even if the juvenile does not hold a driving licence, when endorsement is required by law such an order must still be made. This operates as an order that any licence which the juvenile may subsequently obtain must be endorsed until the relevant time limit has expired. Similarly, a disqualification will serve to prevent the juvenile obtaining a driving licence, including in situations where no licence has been held so far. These items should also appear on police records of previous findings of guilt and any printout supplied by the Driver and Vehicle Licensing Agency (DVLA).
- The general rule is that there can be no discretionary disqualification unless the offence is endorsable. But courts may impose disqualification in respect of offences of taking a motor vehicle without consent, stealing a motor vehicle or going equipped for the theft of a vehicle (often committed by juveniles)—despite the fact that these offences are not in themselves endorsable.
- When a court convicts an offender of any road traffic offence—for which disqualification is obligatory or discretionary—it can order the defendant to be disqualified until he or she passes a driving test. As long as there is no other disqualification in force, the defendant is entitled to drive but must display L-plates and be supervised. This is, of course, subject to a juvenile being of the minimum age to hold a licence to drive—16 for motorcycles and 17 for cars. If the relevant provisional licence condition is breached then a charge of driving whilst disqualified can be brought (e.g. where a juvenile subject to such a disqualification drives without 'L' plates or supervision).
- The Road Traffic (New Drivers) Act 1995 came into effect in 1997. A main object of the Act is to reduce the level of accidents and injuries amongst newly qualified drivers. This is achieved by mandatory revocation by the DVLA of a driving licence where a new driver accumulates six or more penalty points on his or her

---

[3] For an overview, see *Introduction to Road Traffic Offences*, Winston Gordon, Philip Cuddy and Andy Wesson (Waterside Press, 1998)

driving licence within two years beginning with the day on which he or she first passed a test to drive any class of motor vehicle. He or she is then only entitled to hold—and drive in accordance with—a provisional licence until a re-test is passed.

Although the youth court does not order the revocation, as a matter of good practice the licence holder should be advised that the penalty points imposed will lead to revocation under the Act. Once notified by the court, the DVLA will send a revocation letter to the defendant which will take effect from five days after the date of issue. The 1995 Act is intended to introduce a road safety measure and magistrates should be alert to the fact that some defendants may encourage them to impose a short disqualification to circumvent that legislation. A short disqualification (which will not result in any penalty points being endorsed on the licence or notified to the DVLA) may be more attractive to the defendant than a re-test. Generally, youth courts will, in any event, weigh the implications of short periods of disqualification for juveniles against the need for public protection through road safety.

PART THREE

Explanatory Charts

YOUTH COURT SENTENCING FRAMEWORK

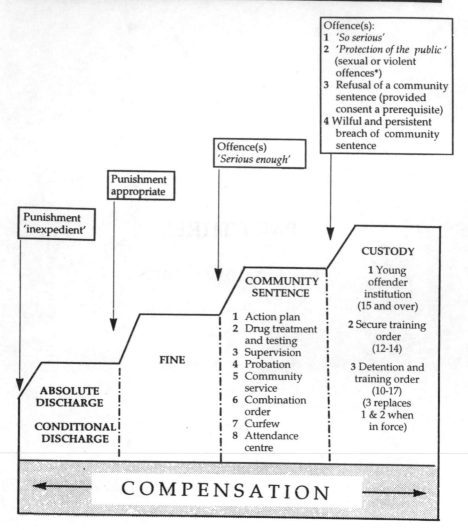

Offence(s):
1 *'So serious'*
2 *'Protection of the public '* (sexual or violent offences*)
3 Refusal of a community sentence (provided consent a prerequisite)
4 Wilful and persistent breach of community sentence

Offence(s) *'Serious enough'*

Punishment appropriate

Punishment 'inexpedient'

CUSTODY

1 Young offender institution (15 and over)

2 Secure training order (12-14)

3 Detention and training order (10-17) (3 replaces 1 & 2 when in force)

COMMUNITY SENTENCE

1 Action plan
2 Drug treatment and testing
3 Supervision
4 Probation
5 Community service
6 Combination order
7 Curfew
8 Attendance centre

FINE

ABSOLUTE DISCHARGE

CONDITIONAL DISCHARGE

COMPENSATION

Chart 1

* All references in this handbook to *sexual* or *violent* offences are to these offences as defined in the Criminal Justice Act 1991: see page 137

It should be noted that other forms of order may be appropriate in an individual case but do not fit readily into the basic sentencing framework, e.g. reparation orders, parenting orders, sex-offender orders. These items and their individual purpose/criteria, are dealt with at appropriate points in the text.

Chart 2: Some Procedures Affected by Age

Age last birthday	10	11	12	13	14	15	16	17
Mode of trial *Chapter 6*	A	A	A	A	A	A	A	A
Parental Responsibility *Chapter 8*	B	B	B	B	B	B	C	C
Remand on bail (with or without conditions) *Chapter 7*	C	C	C	C	C	C	C	C
Remand in local authority accommodation with or without security requirement *Chapter 7*	C	C	C	C	C	C	C	–
Remand to prison establishment *Chapter 7*	–	–	–	–	–	C male	C male	C
Remand to police custody before a finding of guilt *Chapter 7*	–	–	–	–	–	D	D	E
Committal to Crown Court for sentence *Chapter 8*	–	–	–	–	–	C	C	C
Guilty plea by post *Chapter 5*	–	–	–	–	–	–	C	C

A   Only in relation to 'Grave Crimes': see pp.55-59. If charged with homicide (including causing death by dangerous driving) a juvenile must be committed for trial at the Crown Court. See also *Juveniles in the Adult Court*: p.53

B   Duty to bind over parents/guardians 'if desirable'. Duty to order parents/guardians to pay financial orders unless unreasonable.

C   Order/procedure available.

D   Available for up to 24 hours.

E   Available for up to 72 hours.

Explanatory Notes for Chart 3 opposite

A   Orders which can be made by the youth court.

B   Minimum four months, maximum two years. At present 12-14 years inclusive only.
Will be replaced by detention and training order when in force.

C   Orders which can be made by the youth court, when the maximum term is one year in aggregate for two or more indictable offences (a definition which encompasses either way offences). In the Crown Court, the maximum term is two years for a single offence. The minimum term is two months in both courts: see, generally, Chapter 8.
Will be replaced by detention and training order when in force.

D   Minimum four months, maximum 24 months. *Not yet in force.* *
Will replace detention in a young offender institution and secure training orders.

E   As in 'F' but in respect of a more limited range of offences: see under the heading *Grave crimes* pp.55-59

F   Orders which cannot be made in the youth court, but only following committal for trial at the Crown Court (i.e. trial 'on indictment'): see under the heading *Grave crimes* pp.55-59.

* January 1999

Chart 3 : Summary of Primary Disposals According to Age

Age	U 14	14	15	16	17
Discharge (absolute or conditional)	A	A	A	A	A
Fine	A	A	A	A	A
Compensation	A	A	A	A	A
Deprivation of property	A	A	A	A	A
Probation order				A	A
Community service order				A	A
Combination order				A	A
Supervision order	A	A	A	A	A
Attendance centre	A	A	A	A	A
Reparation order*	A	A	A	A	A
Action plan order*	A	A	A	A	A
Sex offender order	A	A	A	A	A
Parenting order*	A	A	A	A	A
Drug treatment and testing order*				A	A
Secure training order	B	B			
Detention in YOI			C	C	C
Detention and training order	D	D	D	D	D
Detention (s53 CYPA 1933)	E	F	F	F	F

* Being piloted in various areas of the country (January 1999) : see text

Structured Decision-making in the Youth Court

This example of a structured approach is intended to be applied in the light of any national or local guidelines which are in use by the youth panel. The youth court should bear in mind that the principal aim of youth justice is to PREVENT OFFENCES. It must also consider the WELFARE of the individual juvenile and whether to deal with aspects of PARENTAL RESPONSIBILITY.

Stage 1

DECIDE GUIDELINE LEVEL for an average offence of the type in question i.e.
Level 1 Discharge
Level 2 Fine
Level 3 Community sentence
Level 4 Custody

Stage 2

REVIEW in the light of aggravating and mitigating factors affecting the *particular* offence

MAKE INITIAL ASSESSMENT as to sentence level

Stage 3

Do previous convictions/responses to earlier sentences affect this assessment? Was an offence committed whilst on bail?

REVISE ASSESSMENT as to level *if appropriate.*

Stage 4

CONSIDER whether, in certain siuations, any matters concerning the particular offender affect the sentence level: see p.92

REVISE ASSESSMENT as to level *if appropriate*

Arrive at FINAL decision as to which level applies.

Stage 5

CONSIDER sentence WITHIN the level selected
Given the need to prevent offending, to what extent do the following serve to
reduce sentence *within* the level:
Previous good character?
Maturity or immaturity?
Other personal mitigation ('offender mitigation')?
Credit for a guilty plea?
The welfare of the juvenile?

Fines: Consider parental responsibility. Consider local 'guidelines' and
defendant's/parent's etc. individual financial circumstances and revise up or
down as appropriate.
Community sentence: Consider 'restriction of liberty' and 'suitability'.
Consider parental responsibility.
Custody: Consider length of sentence (noting the special rules for violent or
sexual offences).

Whether or not considered at *Stage 3:*
Do previous convictions or responses to earlier sentences affect the above?
Is there an offence on bail?

Stage 6

MAKE SURE COMPENSATION HAS BEEN ADEQUATELY CONSIDERED

Consider parental responsibility.

Stage 7

CONSIDER the TOTALITY PRINCIPLE
Is the final sentence still proportionate to the offence or offences?

If you have departed significantly from the guideline level at *Stage I*, check the
reasons for this.

Continued overleaf

Stage 8

Explain to the juvenile and parents or guardians etc. the way in which the youth court proposes to deal with the case and listen to any representations.

Obtain any appropriate consent, agreement or indication of 'willingness'.

ANNOUNCE SENTENCE including any ancillary orders, e.g. disqualification, endorsement, costs, forfeiture.

Give any statutory (or other appropriate) **REASONS/EXPLANATIONS** 📖✋

Note: *Always seek legal/judicial advice before making a pronouncement in all but the mot straightforward cases:* 📖✋

Chart 4 above: Structured Decision-making in the Youth Court

Extended explanation of *Footnote 2, Chapter 7*

What is described on pp.86-89 in relation to remands to *Secure Accommodation* are transitional arrangements, and give the state of play at the time when this handbook was written. Sections 97 and 98 amend section 23 Children and Young Persons Act 1969 to allow for the implementation of court-ordered secure remands to local authority secure accommodation. However, to quote from the Home Office Introductory Guide to the 1998 Act: 'Commencement - implementation date still to be decided'.

Section 23 as amended by section 97 will allow court-ordered secure remands subject to certain criteria for 12-16 year olds. The category of children and young persons to whom the provisions apply will be determined by the Home Secretary. The criteria are set out in section 23(5).

Section 98 sets out the alternative arrangements which currently apply under section 23 for the remand and committal of 15 and 16 year old boys. To quote directly from the Home Office guide 'At present there is an insufficient number of local authority secure places available to extend the provisions on court-ordered secure remands to all juveniles. This is especially so in the case of 15 and 16 year old boys who can currently be remanded to prison if the criteria in section 23(5) are met'. When implemented, the effect of the amendments in section 98 will be to enable boys aged 15 and 16 to be remanded into local authority secure accommodation if they meet the definition of vulnerability, and if a place in such accommodation has been identified in advance. The vulnerability criteria will apply if a court is of the opinion that, by reasons of his physical or emotional immaturity, or a propensity of his to harm himself, it would be undesirable for him to be remanded to a remand centre or prison. Those who do not meet the criteria will be remanded into custody.

It appears that for some considerable time now, governments have been of the opinion that those aged 16 and under should not be remanded to custody. The reason the provisions have not been implemented has been through lack of appropriate places, which presumably is a matter of funding.

The remand arrangements outlined in *Chapter 7* are already complex and this is made worse by these pending provisions and uncertainity as to their commencement.

Sentences and Orders Available in the Youth Court

SENTENCE	AGE LIMITS	PSR REQUIRED*	CONSENT REQUIRED	MINIMUM	MAXIMUM	COMMENTS
Absolute discharge	None	No	No	n/a	n/a	
Conditional discharge	None	No	No	None	3 years	Not within 2 years of warning, breach of sex offender order or of anti-social behaviour order
Fines	10-13 / 14-17	No / No	No / No	None / None	£250 / £1000	Must reflect seriousness and take financial circumstances of juvenile/parents etc. into account
Compensation (*Primary* or *Ancillary* order)	None	No	No	None	Up to £5,000 per offence	Must take financial circumstances of juvenile/parent into account
Reparation order	10-17	No - but needs 'written report'	No	None	Aggregate 24 hours	*Pilot October 1998 for 18 months* Other qualifications: ▢ ✍
Attendance centre	10-15 / 16-17	No - but good practice / No - but good practice + see comments	No / No	12 hours / 12 hours	24 hours / 36 hours	Can be less than 12 hours for those under 14
Action plan order	10-17	No - but 'written report' needed	No	Order for 3 months if scheme available		Cannot be combined with custody or certain community sentences. *Pilot October 1998 for 18 month:* ▢ ✍

Sentences and Orders Available in the Youth Court (continued)

SENTENCE	AGE LIMITS	PSR REQUIRED*	CONSENT REQUIRED	MINIMUM	MAXIMUM	COMMENTS
Drug treatment and testing order	16-17	No - but good practice	Yes	6 mths	3 years	A community sentence which the court reviews. *Pilots October 1998 for 18 months.*
Supervision order	10-17	No - but good practice	No - unless requirement included	None	3 years	PSR required if additional requirements under CYPA 1969, s.12-12C
Probation	16-17	No - but good practice + see comments	No, unless alcohol/drug treatment	6 months	3 years	PSR required if additional requirements
Community service	16-17	Yes	No	40 hours	240 hours	Assessment for CS is essential
Combination order	16-17	Yes	No	CS 40 hours Probation 12 months	100 hours 3 years	Assessment for CS essential for CS part
Curfew	10-17	No - but good practice	No	None	6 months	2-12 hours in any one day *Notavailable in most areas*
Parental bind over	10-15 *duty* 'if desirable'. Reasons if not.	No	Yes or Fine £1,000	None	Up to £1,000 For 3 years or until offender 18 whichever sooner	Ancillary to sentence
	16-17 *discretion.*	No	Yes or Fine £1,000			Ancillary to sentence

Sentences Available in the Youth Court (continued)

SENTENCE	AGE LIMITS	PSR REQUIRED*	CONSENT REQUIRED	MINIMUM	MAXIMUM	COMMENTS
Parenting order	10-15 (*duty or reasons*) 16-17 (*discretion*)	No need if oral/written information	No	None	12 months 3 months maximum counselling	*Piloting from October 1998 for 18 months*
Detention in young offender institution (Reasons needed)	15-17 (Reasons needed)	Yes.	No	2 months	6 months or maximum for offence if shorter	12 months maximum in aggregate if 2 either way/ indictable offences. *Will be replaced by detention and training order.*
Committal to Crown Court	15-17	No - but good practice	No	2 months imposed by Crown Court	2 years imposed by Crown Court	Offence punishable on indictment. If in custody, to Remand Centre or Prison. *Power will cease when detention and training order in force.*
Secure training order (Reasons needed)	12-14	Yes. Reasons needed	No	6 months	2 years	Subject to qualifications. Seek advice. *Will be replaced by detention and training order.*
Detention and training order	10-17	Yes	No	4 months	24 months	Custodial sentence Subject to qualifications Not in force (possibly summer 1999 for 12-17 year olds).

Notes to Chart 5 above: Sentences Available in the Youth Court

- See p.66 for the circumstances in which PSRs can be declared 'unnecessary' and note the important rider concerning juveniles

- Drug treatment and testing orders (when in force) are supervised only by a probation officer. They can involve resident treatment: 🖳 👆

- Detention and training orders (when in force) can only be imposed for periods of 4, 6, 8, 10, 18 or 24 months, subject to the maximum for the offence in question.

- Parenting orders (when in force) can consist of two elements:

  – Counselling/guidance sessions
  – A requirement to exercise control over the child's behaviour

Also

  – Where the juvenile is 16 or 17 there is a discretion to make the order.
  – The maximum counselling element is for three months with not more than one session per week.
  – The provisions are subject to qualifications: 🖳 👆.

Supervision orders

  – The conditions can include reparation for up to 90 days (when in force): 🖳 👆
  – The youth court can resentence on breach
  – The youth court can also include a requirement to live in local authority accommodation in certain circumstances, e.g. where the offence was committed during the period when a supervision order was in force: 🖳 👆.

Children Who Break the Law or 'Everybody Does It'
Sarah Curtis

What are persistent young offenders, children of 14 to 16 or even younger, really like? What do they think about when they steal or rob people? Why do they think they are always getting into trouble?

In *Children Who Break the Law* eleven young people talk about all aspects of their lives, from their families to the schools most of them do not attend, and they describe what they want from the future. Sarah Curtis, who has been a youth court and family court magistrate in Inner London for over 20 years also records interviews with some of their parents. Did the parents collude in their children's law-breaking or did the exercise parental responsibility? What do they think might have stopped their children from getting into trouble?

Next the book explores the ways in which children like Tyrrell, Jason, Jacquie, and the 'terrible twins', Robert and Cliff (all names have been changed for confidentiality) could have been diverted from criminality. Sarah Curtis argues that we know *how* to prevent juvenile offending but successive governments subscribe to a rhetoric of punishment and will not give adequate resources to prevention (the Government's new flagship criteria as set out in the Crime and Disorder Act 1998). She describes projects in the community of proven benefit which support parents, schemes which reach teenagers *on their own wavelength*, ways to reintegrate disruptive children into school and methods of teaching the difference between right and wrong, of inculcating good citizenship. Finally she considers the proposals in the Youth Justice and Criminal Evidence Bill for referral orders before calling for reform of the youth court, suggestions which go well beyond those of government.

This vivid, combative yet constructive book is informative for professionals in the field of criminal justice and for general readers, disturbed by press reporting of youth crime, alike. It is rare that the views of offenders under the age of 18 have been recorded and even rarer for their parents to be asked their opinions. *Children Who Break the Law* combines first-class journalism with expert knowledge, to make a book which is wise and practical.

Sarah Curtis has been youth court and family court magistrate since 1978. She began her career in journalism on *The Times Educational Supplement* and *The Times*, going on to edit *Adoption & Fostering* (the BAAF journal), and the *Journal of the Royal Society of Arts*. She has worked in community relations and was co-author of a pioneering series of strip-cartoon stories for teenagers about health and social issues. Her 1989 book, *Juvenile Offending: Prevention Through Intermediate Treatment,* was highly praised. She reviews novels regularly for *The Times Literary Supplement* and is editing the *Journals of Woodrow Wyatt*, the first volume of which appeared in 1998.

ISBN 1 872 870 76 7 £16 plus £1.50 p&p
Scheduled for publication in June 1999.

Criminal Justice 2000: Strategies for a New Century
Michael Cavadino, Iain Crow and James Dignan

What is the nature of New Labour criminal justice policy? What strategic options does the government have for dealing with the problems of crime and punishment—and where is it likely to take us in future? This timely book analyses past and present policies in British criminal justice and distills a set of three broad options for its future, including a principled approach which seeks to protect the human rights of offenders and victims by means such as rehabilitation, reintegration and restorative justice. 1999 ISBN Paperback 1 872 870 77 5. £20

Restoring Respect for Justice
Martin Wright

This innovative work takes the author's analysis of restorative justice to new heights—by way of an imaginative 'Symposium' of experts. Fully referenced and encompassing an account of developments in this field since his acclaimed earlier work, *Justice for Victims and Offenders: A Restorative Response to Crime* (Waterside Press, 1996). 1999 ISBN 1 872 878 3. £18

Introduction to Criminology
Russell Pond

A basic guide—written with people working in criminal justice particularly in mind. 1999 ISBN 1 872 870 42 2. £13.50

Crime and Banishment: Nuisance and Exclusion in Social Housing
Elizabeth Burney

A ground-breaking look at the use of civil and administrative powers by social landlords as a means of preventing crime, disorder and 'anti-social behavour'. 1999 ISBN 1 872 870 79 1. £16

Conflict Resolution A Foundation Guide
Susan Stewart

Of interest to people who deal with disputes of all kinds—including through mediation and alternative dispute resolution procedures. 1998 ISBN 1 872 870 65 1. £13.50

Human Rights and the Courts: Bringing Justice Home
Paul Ashcroft, Fiona Barrie, Chris Bazell, Audrey Damazer, Richard Powell, George Tranter. Edited by Bryan Gibson
This highly succesful work was divised in consultation with the Lord Chancellor's Department, Judicial Studies Board and Justices' Clerks' Society ready for implementation of the Human Rights Act 1998 (the main text of which is included in this excellent book). 1999 ISBN 1 872 870 80 5. £10

Children Who Break the Law: or Everybody Does It
Sarah Curtis
A very readable book which records at first hand young people talking about their chaotic lives, hopes for the future and anxieties—where possible recording their parents' views also. Sarah Curtis points out that *we do know* how to prevent much juvenile offending through community projects of proven benefit and other tried and tested means of reintegrating children in trouble with the law into schools, colleges, communities and careers. 1999 ISBN 1 872 870 76 7. £18

Going Straight After Crime and Punishment
Compiled by Angela Devlin and Bob Turney
Foreword by Jack Straw, Home Secretary
Going Straight looks at a range of criminals who have changed their way of life. They include famous, notorious, creative and ordinary people who were prepared to talk about the turning point in their lives—the events which caused them to leave crime behind. Their candid explanations about how they rebuilt their lives—often full of remorse for their victims and determined to repay something to their communities—are challenging, illuminating and a cause for optimism. 1999 ISBN 1 872 870 66X. £18 (Royalties payable to UNLOCK)

Juvenile Delinquents and Young People in Danger in an Open Environment Willie McCarney (Ed.)
'Contains some extremely interesting findings' *The Law.* 'I recommend this edition' *The Magistrate.* Produced under the auspices of the International Association of Juvenile and Family Court Magistrates with support from the European Commission, this highly praised international survey of youth justice is the first English version of *Jeunes Delinquants et Jeunes en Danger en Millieu Ouvert* (Erès, Toulouse). It comprises a series of reports about legal frameworks and youth justice practice across Europe—plus a special section on youth justice in Brazil. 1996 ISBN 1 872 870 39 2. £20